GOD HAS NEVER FAILED ME,

BUT HE'S SURE SCARED ME
TO DEATH A FEW TIMES

GOD HAS NEVER FAILED ME,
BUT HE'S SURE SCARED ME TO DEATH A FEW TIMES

Stan Toler

David C Cook®

transforming lives together

GOD HAS NEVER FAILED ME, BUT
HE'S SURE SCARED ME TO DEATH A FEW TIMES
Published by David C. Cook
4050 Lee Vance View
Colorado Springs, CO 80918 U.S.A.

David C. Cook Distribution Canada
55 Woodslee Avenue, Paris, Ontario, Canada N3L 3E5

David C. Cook U.K., Kingsway Communications
Eastbourne, East Sussex BN23 6NT, England

David C. Cook and the graphic circle C logo
are registered trademarks of Cook Communications Ministries.

Unless otherwise indicated, all scripture quotations are taken from the *Holy
Bible, New International Version*®. *NIV*®. Copyright © 1973, 1978, 1984 by
International Bible Society. Used by permission of Zondervan Publishing House.
All rights reserved. Scripture quotations marked KJV are taken from the King James
Version of the Bible. (Public Domain.) The author has added
italics in Scripture quotations for emphasis.

LCCN 2009905009
ISBN 978-1-4347-6595-6
eISBN 978-1-4347-0041-4

© 1995 Stan Toler
First edition published by Honor Books® in 1995
© Stan Toler, ISBN 1-56292-130-4

The Team: Don Pape, Amy Kiechlin, Sarah Schultz,
Jack Campbell, Caitlyn York, and Karen Athen
Cover Design/Illustration: Luke Flowers

Printed in the United States of America
Second Edition 2009

1 2 3 4 5 6 7 8 9 10

052709

To my mother, Loretta, who taught me at an early age the importance of a relationship with Jesus Christ.

Be strong and courageous. Do not be afraid or terrified because of them, for the LORD your God goes with you; he will never leave you nor forsake you. (Deut. 31:6)

CONTENTS

Discover More Online

FOR DISCUSSION QUESTIONS, VISIT

WWW.DAVIDCCOOK.COM/GODHASNEVERFAILEDME

ACKNOWLEDGMENTS

Special thanks …

To the Trinity Church of the Nazarene family—
your support, encouragement, and prayers mean
so much.

To Barbara Johnson, for encouraging me to write
this book and to stick with my title.

To Jim Wilcox, the SNU "Grammar Hammer,"
my tennis partner, and the man with the red
pen for wise editorial guidance and helpful
suggestions.

To Mechelle Fain, for countless hours in front of
a computer typing and retyping the manuscript.
Bless you for your ability to read my handwriting!

To Derl Keefer, for research assistance and creative
ideas.

To Mom, Dad, Terry, and Mark—I love you more
than words can express.

To all sources unknown—I would love to give
credit where credit is due, but after nearly thirty
years of ministry, I don't remember. Let me know,
and I will credit you in my next printing.

To my wife, Linda, for reading rough draft
chapters and for verifying the accuracy of my
stories.

To Talmadge Johnson, "G. I. Barber," brother
beloved. Thanks for your confidence in me.

To Charles and Stephanie Wetzel, for insightful
suggestions and content review. What a team!

To Martha Bolton, for witty ideas, friendship, and
editorial insights.

To my sons, Seth and Adam, for giving me
permission to tell your stories (and for serving as
proofreaders!).

You are loved.

Stan Toler
Ephesians 3:20–21

FOREWORD

The title of this book would make a best seller, even if the material were not captivating. Stan has the ability to bond laughter with the solid truth of the Scriptures in a way that makes joy erupt in my life over God's faithfulness.

With the story in chapter 1 about God's provision for us, I sensed that *warm, fuzzy wrapping* of God dropping His canvas of love over us. Sometimes we are more aware of it than other times.

The sparkling stories of incidents revealing God's care for us come through so clearly in Stan's writing. Somehow the small, almost trite situations shine through and become like lights brightly outlining a darkened pathway.

This book is such an encouragement, even in heavy circumstances, reminding us that God did not begin to love us because of what we were, and that He will go on loving us in spite of what we are. The grace of God is so poured out on us with Stan's wise counsel.

We know the word *encourage* means "to fill the heart," and Stan does a superb job of using Scripture and anecdotes to truly "fill the heart." The blend of spiritual truths—plus insights learned from a life of service to God—makes this book rich in wisdom and exhortation.

I recently began collecting figurines of angels, such as Gabriel holding up his trumpet. After reading this book, I went out and bought four more angels to place around my home, just to remind me that hope is ahead of us. We have an *endless hope,* not a *hopeless end,* and this book challenges me to keep that thought preeminent: looking for His blessed appearing.

Joyfully, with love,
Barbara Johnson

PREFACE

Anyone who first meets Stan Toler knows immediately that he is an original. No one else I know has the same kind of wit, charm, and positive outlook on life that he does. And he is also one of the funniest men I have ever met. Stan has the uncanny ability to see the humor in any situation, capture it in his imagination, and then recount it with all the grace and style of a southern storyteller. I have been glad to call Stan my good friend and colleague for more than thirty years.

What you cannot tell when you first meet Stan is that he has experienced some genuinely difficult times, times that would knock the humor out of someone else the way the wind gets knocked out of you when you land flat on your back.

But Stan has an unsinkable spirit. He also possesses keen insight. In this book, he shares many of his observations and insights—loaded with humor, of course. You will find yourself laughing one minute and crying the next. In the end, you will come to share his outlook. You will begin to see humor in life's circumstances. And as Scripture says, "A merry heart doeth good like a medicine" (Prov. 17:22 KJV).

John C. Maxwell
Founder of INJOY
Atlanta, Georgia

INTRODUCTION

God Has Never Failed Me, but He's Sure Scared Me to Death a Few Times is a book about the faithfulness of God. Within its pages you will find humorous and inspirational stories of God's power very much at work in the world.

Leslie Miller of *USA Today* once stated, "When it comes to religion, the USA is a land of believers. A new *USA Today*/CNN/Gallup Poll reveals that 96 percent of Americans believe in God."[1]

It's almost hard to believe that statistic, considering how many people seem to try to make it without Him. Perhaps J. I. Packer was right when he said, "Our expectations of seeing the power of God transforming people's lives are not … as high as they should be."

One of the best ways God changes us is through the impact of humor. I learned this as a young teen attending the Fifth Avenue Church in Columbus, Ohio. I often heard my pastor, the Rev. C. O. Walters, ask the question, "Is everybody happy? If so, say Amen!" What an impact this had on my spiritual life—a minister who believes in laughter!

Maybe the importance of humor in our spiritual life is at the heart of a story I heard about a three-year-old boy who listened attentively to a Sunday morning message. When he was asked about what he had learned, the child responded, "Jesus died so that we could have ever-laughing life!" And you know what? He is right! Salvation and everlasting life certainly include joy and laughter.

Humor truly is a godsend. Oswald Chambers called humor "the lubricant of missionary life." Laughter is very much a part of my faith life. I hope it is also a part of yours. When we dismiss laughter from the pulpit, the pew, and everyday life, we miss God's best for us in Christian experiences.

Humor is to life what shock absorbers are to automobiles.

My love of humor has always been paired with a simple faith in God's ability to perform miracles. As a child, I was often encouraged by the words affixed to the wall in the choir loft of my home church: "Jesus Never Fails." I accepted this at face value and have never ceased to believe that "God can do anything but fail!"

It is our prayer that this book will inspire you and many others to renewed faith in God's ability to do the impossible. May the words of the prophet Isaiah challenge your faith and calm your fears.

> *Fear not, for I have redeemed you; I have summoned you by name; you are mine. When you pass through the waters, I will be with you; and when you pass through the rivers, they will not sweep over you. When you walk through the fire, you will not be burned; the flames will not set you ablaze. For I am the LORD, your God, the Holy One of Israel, your Savior; I give Egypt for your ransom, Cush and Seba in your stead. Since you are precious and honored in my sight, and because I love you, I will give men in exchange for you, and people in exchange for your life. Do not be afraid, for I am with you; I*

will bring your children from the east and gather you from the west. (Isa. 43:1–5)

What God did for the children of Israel, He can and will do for you. God has never failed me, and He will never fail you.

You are loved,
Stan Toler

CHAPTER 1

Pinto Beans and Fried Bologna—

Now That's a Feast of Faith

We do not know what to do. (2 Chron. 20:12)

Growing up in the hills of West Virginia impacted my life tremendously. My dad was a coal miner, and we lived in a coal-mining community—Baileysville, an unincorporated town. Of course, most towns in West Virginia are still unincorporated. And the population of Baileysville was down to sixty as of 1994, so I guess it will never be incorporated! In fact, it's so small that Main Street is a cul-de-sac. But it is my hometown!

Californians love to brag about being able to go to the mountains to snow ski and the ocean to sunbathe in the same day. Well, in Baileysville, we had our own definition of the good life. If you lived on the side of the mountain, you could cross the river anytime, any day, on an old-fashioned swinging bridge!

My Saturdays were spent at the Wyoming Company Store. While Mom and Dad made purchases with coal-mining dollars, I took charge of watching my brothers, Terry and Mark. That wasn't difficult if you knew what to do. We eagerly peered at the black-and-white television sets in the furniture department. Programs such as *Fury, Sky King,* and *My Friend Flicka* seemed so real to us!

Our small white frame house was located on the side of Baileysville Mountain. We had a well nearby that provided ample water and a pot-bellied coal stove to keep us warm (as long as you remembered to put the coal in it!).

I have heard that someone can be described as a "redneck" if his bathroom requires a flashlight and shoes. Well, our house had three rooms and a path to the little house out back. But it was our home, and I loved it—no matter how pink it made my neck.

One of the saddest days of my childhood was a Saturday morning when we returned home from a visit to the company store to see our tiny home engulfed in flames. We lost everything. I cried for days.

Years later, Pastor Richard Grindstaff told us that as the house burned to the ground, Dad put his arm around him and said, "The Lord giveth, and the Lord taketh away. Blessed be the name of the Lord!"

PUT THE ROADKILL ON THE TABLE, AND CALL THE KIDS FOR SUPPER!

By the time I was eleven years old, we had moved to Columbus, Ohio, in search of a better life. My dad, only thirty-one years old, had already broken his back three times in the coal mines and was suffering from the dreaded miners' disease "black lung." But we were happy and almost always had pinto beans, cornbread, and fried bologna for supper. (That's right, only later did we call it *dinner!*)

Christmas Day 1961 will always be one of the most wonderful, life-changing days in my memory bank. It had been a long, hard winter with lots of snow and cold weather. Times were tough! Dad had been laid off from construction work, our food supply had dwindled to nothing, and we had closed off most of the house in order to cut down our high utility bills.

This epiphany really began Christmas Eve when Mom noted that we had no food for Christmas Day and no hope of getting any. That was difficult for me to understand. We were used to Mom calling out, "Pinto beans, cornbread, and fried bologna. Come and get it!" But now we didn't even have that. There was no food in the house!

Mom suggested that it was time for us to accept a handout from the government commodities department, so—reluctantly—Dad loaded Terry, Mark, and me into our old Plymouth, and we headed downtown. When we got there, we stood in line with hundreds of others for what seemed like hours, waiting for government handouts of cheese, dried milk, flour, and dried eggs. Ugh! The wind was cold, and the snow was blowing as we stood there shivering. Finally, Dad could stand it no longer.

"We're going home, boys. God will provide!" he said. We cried, yet we completely trusted Dad's faith in God.

That night, we popped popcorn and opened gifts that we had ordered with Top Value trading stamps that Mom had wisely saved for that purpose. Perhaps some of you are too young to remember Top Value stamps. Back then, almost all grocery stores gave out trading stamps for purchases made. You could save the stamps and fill up Top Value books for redemption. In my day, Top Value provided a catalog that listed the number of books needed for a gift item. So

Mom saved stamps all year long, counted the bounty by November 1, and let us Toler boys pick out our Christmas presents.

Terry got a transistor radio. (He hadn't realized that we had no money to purchase a battery!) I had ordered a miniature Brownie Kodak camera. (That wasn't smart, since we couldn't afford film, either!) And baby brother Mark got a small teddy bear. While none of the gifts was a surprise to us, Mom had carefully and lovingly wrapped each one to be opened Christmas Eve. We were grateful to have anything!

Everyone slept well under Grandma Brewster's handmade quilts that night. While we were fearful of the prospect of the next day without food, we were just happy to be together as a family. (Little did we know that Dad would be in heaven by the following Christmas.)

On Christmas morning, we were all asleep in Mom and Dad's bedroom when suddenly we were startled by a loud knock and a hearty "Merry Christmas!" greeting from people who attended the Fifth Avenue Church. There stood Clair Parsons, Dalmus Bullock, and others with gifts, clothes, and a thirty-day supply of food. (Yes, dried pinto beans, cornmeal, and a huge roll of bologna were included!) Since that day, I have always believed that God will provide, and that God is *never late* when we need a miracle!

> We must bring the presence of God into our families.
> And how do we do that? By praying.
> —Mother Teresa

One of my favorite Bible stories centers around 2 Chronicles 20:12. King Jehoshaphat of Judah found himself in what appeared to be a hopeless situation. He cried out to God, "Our God … we have no power…. We do not know what to do." King Jehoshaphat had just discovered three new enemies. Unfortunately, all three were lined up against the tiny nation of Judah, and King Jehoshaphat realized that he was powerless without God's help. That's the way we felt in the Toler home. The good news for all of us is the same as it was for King Jehoshaphat. God can and will make up the difference.

SEEK THE LORD

> Alarmed, Jehoshaphat resolved to inquire of the LORD, and he proclaimed a fast for all Judah. The people of Judah came together to seek help from the LORD. (2 Chron. 20:3–4)

Jehoshaphat asked God a significant question: "Are you not the God who is in heaven?" (2 Chron. 20:6). In other words, he was saying, "God, if You can take care of this universe and bring order to it, then You can provide for me."

He asked God another question: "Did you not drive out the inhabitants of this land?" (2 Chron. 20:7). He was reminding himself of God's faithfulness in the past. I am beginning to realize that my faith today anchors to the faith that my dad passed on to me with his wisdom: "God will provide." And provide He did for the Tolers!

After Dad's death, God sent a wonderful Kentucky stepfather, Jack Hollingsworth, into our lives. He saw to it that each son of William Aaron Toler had plenty of pinto beans, fried bologna (by the way, he is an expert at cooking it!), cornbread, and a college education. All three boys later became Nazarene ministers.

CONFESS YOUR NEED

We have no power to face this vast army that is attacking us.
(2 Chron. 20:12)

If you want God's help, you must confess your need! The world in which we live is a world of independence. We are taught to look out for number one, to do our own thing, to think for ourselves, and to trust in our own abilities. King Jehoshaphat reminded the people of Judah that "Me-ism" doesn't work here! He confessed that they were inadequate against the three enemies they faced: "Power and might are in your hand" (2 Chron. 20:6).

When I need God's provision, I look up and confess, "God, I am incapable, but You have all the resources for my miracle!"

FOCUS ON GOD, NOT YOUR PROBLEM

We do not know what to do, but our eyes are upon you.
(2 Chron. 20:12)

King Jehoshaphat gave his people a formula for deliverance: "Get your eyes off the problem! Your focus must be on God!"

Living in Oklahoma during tough times as an adult has also strengthened my faith in God. In the mid-1980s, I watched many banks fail; in fact, the FDIC closed so many banks in my hometown of Oklahoma City that I wore a T-shirt that said, "I bank with FDIC!" Agriculture diminished, and oil rigs stopped pumping. But even in the most difficult situations, a simple faith in God and a calm reassurance in the face of insurmountable obstacles resulted in victory.

I will always remember sitting at a table in the Oklahoma City Marriott hotel restaurant on Northwest Expressway and listening to my friend Melvin Hatley, founder of USA Waste Management Company, talk about the collapse of the oil industry and the failure of the old First National Bank downtown. Tears flowed freely, and yet his faith took hold as he discussed God's history of faithfulness. His calm assurance, founded and grounded in a dynamic faith, made all the difference! Today, Melvin is a testimony of the phrase "Tough times don't last, but tough people do!"

Trust and action always work hand in hand. For example, you know the story of Wilbur and Orville Wright. On December 17, 1903, they made history. They defied the law of gravity and flew through the air. Many forget that the concept of flying did not originate with the Wright brothers. In fact, several years before the brothers flew their motorized plane at Kitty Hawk, scientists had discovered that flying was possible. While others remained skeptical, the Wright brothers believed the formulas and designed their own plane. When they achieved "first flight," they demonstrated the importance of trusting the facts and taking action in order to experience results.

The same is true for Christians. We can know a lot about God and the Bible, but until we relax in faith and believe in the promises of God, we will be disappointed.

I love the story that my former professor Dr. Amos Henry used to tell about D. L. Moody. Apparently, Moody was on a ship crossing the Atlantic Ocean one night when the vessel caught on fire, and all on board formed a bucket brigade to pass ocean water to the scene of the fire. One man in the line turned and said, "Mr. Moody, don't you think we should retire from the line and go down and pray?"

"You can go pray if you want to," Moody replied, "but I'm going to pray while I pass the buckets." What great insight! God wants to see if you mean business, so *pray while you work.*

Just think, if Jesus had thought prayer was the only thing He needed to do and had remained on His knees in the garden of Gethsemane instead of getting up and following God's plan for His life, there never would have been a Calvary.

RELAX IN FAITH

One of the great things about faith is that it helps you persevere. There's a story about two men who were climbing a particularly difficult mountain when one of them suddenly fell down a crevasse five hundred feet deep.

"Are you all right, Bert?" called the man at the top of the crevasse.

"I'm still alive, thank goodness, Fred," came the reply.

"Here, grab this rope," said Fred, throwing a rope down to Bert.

"I can't grab it," shouted Bert. "My arms are broken."

"Well, fit it around your legs."

"I'm afraid I can't do that either," said Bert. "My legs are broken."

"Put the rope in your mouth," shouted Fred.

So Bert put the rope in his mouth and Fred began to haul him to safety: four hundred ninety feet ... four hundred feet ... three hundred feet ... two hundred feet ... one hundred feet ... fifty feet ... and then Fred called out, "Hey, Bert, how are you doing?"

Bert replied, "I'm fine ... Uh oh!"

Don't let go of the rope, my friend! As Dr. Steve Brown says, "Tie a knot and hang on!"

You will not have to fight this battle. Take up your positions; stand firm and see the deliverance the LORD will give you. (2 Chron. 20:17)

It's interesting that this particular verse is the middle verse of the entire Old Testament. It is like a pregnant pause for the believer. This concept, "stand firm," is like going into the batter's box during a World Series baseball game with a great pitcher on the mound, digging in, and saying, "I don't care how fast you throw that ball, I'm anchored here, and you can't move me!" King Jehoshaphat said, "Stand your ground and remain calm—God is going to help us."

Of course, that's easier said than done. Harmon Schmelzenbach, a missionary to Africa, often holds audiences spellbound with his story about a huge python that uncoiled itself from the rafters and then wrapped itself around his body while he was kneeling to pray.

The python is known for its ability to kill its victim by squeezing it to death. Schmelzenbach stated that Isaiah 30:15 instantly flooded his mind: "In repentance and rest is your salvation, in quietness and trust is your strength, but you would have none of it." With the huge snake wrapped around his body, he testified that he felt the calm assurance that God was in control. Harmon remained perfectly still and prayed as never before!

If he had moved a muscle, no doubt the giant python would have constricted and killed him. But Schmelzenbach reported that the snake slowly uncoiled itself and went back to the rafters. I don't know if Schmelzenbach now prays with one eye open or not, but one thing's for certain: No one can convince him that there isn't power in the promises of God.

We can depend on God. Did you know that we have more than seven thousand promises in Scripture to stand on? Not only that, but you can stand on the character of God! God has never lost a battle. Why not resign as general manager of the universe, eat a bowl of beans and cornbread, and relax in faith?

GIVE GOD THANKS BEFORE YOUR MIRACLE

King Jehoshaphat began to appoint those who could sing. "As they began to sing and praise, the LORD set ambushes against the men of Ammon and Moab and Mount Seir who were invading Judah, and they were defeated" (2 Chron. 20:22). Do you get the picture? Three armies of bloodthirsty warriors with overwhelming strength and weaponry lined up against tiny Judah, and the king called the choir to sing! Talk about faith. That day they claimed victory!

God is faithful now in the twenty-first century, just as He was in the days of ancient Israel. During the Second World War, the Allies experienced a very difficult time. The British had just suffered a terrible defeat at Dunkirk, losing almost all of their military supplies during the evacuation of their soldiers. France had been conquered, and the United Sates had not yet entered the war. The island nation of England stood alone against the Axis powers.

Prime Minister Winston Churchill knew he had to bolster the courage and the determination of his people. He needed to make a speech—an inspiring speech—that would rally the citizens. On Sunday evening, June 2, 1940, Churchill was in his Cabinet Room at 10 Downing Street. His secretary, Mary Shearburn, was poised at the typewriter. Dictating, Churchill paced from the fireplace to the velvet-draped windows and back again. Slowly his speech emerged onto the typed page. Often he would rip the sheet from the machine only to begin anew. It was late, and the room was cold in the night air. The prime minister's voice had now grown hoarse and faint. His head bowed, and he sobbed, for he did not know what to say. Silence. A minute passed, maybe two. It seemed like an eternity. Abruptly his head rose and his voice trumpeted; he spoke as a man with authority. The thought descended upon him, as from an angel above: "We shall *never* surrender!"

Perhaps those words did come from an angel. Who knows? All we know is that God is faithful. Regardless of how scary or how seemingly hopeless our mission may be, He does not forsake us. All we have to do is trust—placing our fears and our failures in His hands. He will not let us down.[2]

Back in 1853, during the California Gold Rush, a young man from Bavaria came to San Francisco, bringing with him some rolls of canvas. He was twenty-four years old at the time, and he planned to sell the canvas to the gold miners to use for tents. Then the profits from his sales would finance his own digging for gold. However, as he headed toward the Sierra Nevada mountains, he met one of the gold miners. When he told the miner his plans, the miner said, "It won't work. It's a waste of your time. Nobody will buy your canvas for tents. That's not what we need."

The young man prayed within. Then he got his answer.

The gold miner went on: "You should have brought pants. That's what we need—durable pants! Pants don't wear worth a hoot up there in the diggings. Can't get a pair strong enough." Right then, the young man from Bavaria decided to turn the rolls of canvas into pants—blue pants—that would survive the rigors of the gold-mining camps. He had a harness maker reinforce the pockets with copper studs, and the pants sold like hotcakes!

By the way, the name of the young man from Bavaria was Levi Strauss. And he called the new pants "Levi's"! So far, about 900 million pairs of Levi's have been sold throughout the world, and they are one of the few items of apparel whose style has remained basically unchanged for more than 130 years.[3]

It is amazing that a style of pants could endure for over a century. How much more incredible is the unwavering faithfulness of God. I'll never forget the simple hope in His faithfulness that I learned at home. My own father modeled that faith in God before us, trudging home in the snow from the coal mines, face darkened with coal dust, lunch bucket jangling, whistling the old tune "His Eye Is on the Sparrow."

Why should I feel discouraged?
Why should the shadows come?
Why should my heart be lonely
And long for heaven and home?
When Jesus is my portion?
My constant friend is He.
His eye is on the sparrow,
And I know He watches me![4]

—Civilla D. Martin

Yes, the God who sits on a throne in heaven is interested in you! If He tends to the lilies of the fields and attends the funeral of a baby sparrow (and He *does*), He surely will provide for you!

CHAPTER 2

Who Signed Me Up for the Whole Day?

As parents, we think it's hard on us when Junior hops off for that first day of school, but think about the trauma for him!

Six-year-old Brian was more than a little bit anxious on his first day of first grade. Having survived kindergarten, this excited young scholar felt pretty confident that, given time, he would master the new demands of "higher education." But by about 10:30, he felt the day was dragging on. When the bell finally sounded at noon, he couldn't have been more pleased. He followed all his classmates out the door, down the hall, and into the playground … then he kept right on walking toward the gate to freedom.

His alert teacher, noticing that he was trying to leave the school grounds, rushed to intercept the potential delinquent.

"Brian," she said when she finally caught up to him, "why are you leaving school so early?"

"I heard the bell, Miss Stewart, so I'm going home," Brian said, quite self-assured.

"But Brian," she replied, "you're in the first grade now. School doesn't get out until three o'clock. Didn't you know?"

"No," Brian said, lowering his head, embarrassed and confused. Then, after a long pause of deep thought, he looked back up at Miss Stewart and said, "What I want to know is *who signed me up for the whole day?*"

Such began Brian's long journey of coping with the stress that life throws at us—and often when we least expect it.

According to Dr. David Stroop, stress has replaced infection this century as the number one cause of terminal disease. In his book *Self Talk*, Dr. Stroop maintained,

> 40 million Americans suffer from stress-caused
>   allergies
> 30 million suffer from stress-related illnesses
> 25 million are dealing daily with hypertension
>   brought on by stress, and
> 20 million more cases of ulcers aggravated by
>   stress are now being reported.

Let's face it—we're worrying ourselves to death. If you don't believe me, check out the latest sales figures for Tums and Rolaids.

It's important for us to get a handle on pressure, stress, tension, anxiety—whatever you want to label it—so that instead of wasting our lives in a needless war of nerves, we will be able to focus our energy and time on building God's kingdom.

How do you know whether you're reaching stress overload? There are plenty of signs to watch for. The following are just a few:

You Know You're on Stress Overload When:

1. You start talking to your plants—for advice.
2. You order crushed Tagamet on your frozen yogurt.
3. You've chewed all your own fingernails and now you're eyeing your spouse's.
4. You've developed a twitch ... to go with your other four.
5. You wake up at 3:00 a.m. and start working on your income taxes ... in July.
6. You start making simple spelling errors ... like in your name.
7. You find that the startling noise of your neighbors fluffing a pillow makes you jump.
8. Your dog posts a sign that says BEWARE OF HUMAN.
9. You've been watching TV for hours ... and the set isn't even turned on.
10. You have an attack of road rage ... and you haven't even left your driveway.
—Martha Bolton

Undoubtedly, there are as many causes of stress as there are people in our society—and sometimes the cause of our stress *is* the people in our own little circle of society.

WHAT MADE YOUR STRESS CROSS OVER INTO DISTRESS?

If you had to pinpoint three or four things in your life that cause you the most frustration, what would they be? Finances? Automobile problems? Plumbing? Your kids? Being on the waiting end of "call waiting"?

When asked that question, students usually say they get stressed about their grades in a certain course. Company owners may feel stressed about the budget's bottom line, while their employees feel stressed about being in the unemployment line. Lovers get stressed about their relationships, while loners feel stressed because they don't have a romantic relationship. Politicians stress out about the polls, and the public stresses out about the politicians. Police officers are stressed about the constant danger they experience, while desk workers complain that they don't have enough adventure in their lives.

Lloyd Ogilvie stated in his book *Ask Him Anything* that when you boil down all the individual causes of stress, there are six universals that capture almost all of them: change, conflict, criticism, concerns, compression, and conscience.[5] Any one of these can be debilitating, but a combination of two or more can be absolutely destructive.

I'm trying to keep up with the Joneses, but every time I catch up, they just refinance!

My son Seth played on the Southern Nazarene University baseball team with a young man named Craig Shepperd. Craig was born with a heart defect that gave him only a fifty-fifty chance of survival through his first year of life. But he was a battler, and he did not have his first open-heart surgery until he was four. Eleven years later, he had to have a second surgery. According to Murray Evans, staff writer for *The Sunday Oklahoman,* Craig's fight continued beyond simply the urge to survive:

> Immediately after undergoing his second open-heart surgery, Craig Shepperd couldn't talk, but he could write. So he scribbled a question any fifteen-year-old boy who just endured such an operation might ask: "Can I play baseball?"

> A month later, Shepperd joined his Mustang High School team for preseason drills. Four years later, his baseball skills are helping pay his way through college.

> "This child started with a life-threatening problem, and now he's pitching baseball. I'm amazed the he's gotten to this point," said Dr. Jerry Razook, a cardiologist at Children's Hospital in Oklahoma who has worked with Shepperd and his family since shortly after the player's birth. "Craig will have a purpose in life. He is determined."

WHEN BAD BATTLES GOOD, AND GOOD BATTLES BETTER

Sometimes the greatest hurdles in life are the ones we are most likely to meet successfully—but only if we don't let stress get the better of us. Little doubts often cause those gnawing feelings in our hearts (our "gut") that makes them burn, often keeping us awake at night until we reach for the closest antacid tablet—or two or three or four. They raise our blood pressure and lower our productivity. These doubts arise in our relationships—close and distant, personal and professional, dear and dreary—whether those relationships are with us, without us, and even within us.

I'M OKAY, BUT I'VE GOT SOME DOUBTS ABOUT YOU

It is during these moments of doubt that we also experience perhaps another major cause of stress: judgment. Whether it's constructive or otherwise, it doesn't matter—nobody likes to be judged. It raises the hair on the back of our necks (if we've got some left) and causes us to put up our defensive coping mechanisms, even if we are doing the judging. Self-judgment—censure—is so easy to do when one is a perfectionist. Nothing is ever good enough; the perfectionist lives in a constant state of limbo between satisfaction and an overshadowing fear of failure. Also, external denouncement often comes into play. People who feel some kind of competition may become envious, striving to lower the position of the perfectionist in order to achieve a higher level themselves.

I once knew a boy named John whose story demonstrates the impact of judgment and criticism. When John was playing high school basketball, his coach offered him an unbalanced proportion of negative criticism. The coach had been an outstanding college basketball player himself, drafted by an NBA team. Yet he was never happy with anything John did—perhaps because he didn't make it in the professional ranks, or maybe because he was simply a perfection-ist. But for whatever reason, it seemed that everything John did in practice and in the games wasn't done well enough. To make matters worse, the coach had a fiery temper that resulted in language directed at John that he had never before heard. John might have improved under an encouraging coach, but the negativity of this coach ate away at John's confidence. He eventually gave up playing basketball and never felt the same about the game again.

How'd This Bull's-Eye Get on My Back?

Harsh criticism always hurts. For any kind of discriminating evaluation or judgment to be effective, it must be solicited and come from a trusted friend or relative. And it takes time to build genuine honesty and confidence into a relationship.

If you want to see the greatest example of grace under the pressure of criticism, look at the life of Jesus. He was a victim of condemnation and blame. And because of His experience, we can be assured that He felt stress just as we do. If you read the last five chapters of the gospel of John, you'll see that Jesus' last days were full of discouragement and stress. Some might think that He never experienced such human frailties because He was the perfect, sinless Son of God. Indeed He was, but even He was also truly tempted at every turn.

Sometimes You Wish You Could Just Rewind

Sometimes discouraging words are unintentionally delivered. Have you ever said something to a friend, a relative, or a complete stranger that he or she took the wrong way? (If you're smiling right now, the answer is probably yes.) Perhaps it happened this morning over a cup of coffee and a doughnut, and immediately, the look on the other person's face made you say to yourself, *I wish I hadn't said that. Could I have that tape back, please?* Maybe the comment was so bad, you're actually even *wearing* that coffee right now. The problem with being misunderstood, of course, is that it often eventually leads to misrepresentation.

Recently, I heard a humorous story that depicts this very point. A minister was trying to pay a compliment to a lady in his church. He brought her up on stage and said, "This woman does a mountain of work behind the scenes. What you actually see her doing is really just the tip of the iceberg. The biggest part of her is at the bottom."

WHEN DID MY DAY BECOME A FORTY-HOUR WEEK?

Stress seems to come at us from every side. It's not always the number or the weight of the responsibilities that debilitate and defeat our spirits. Often, it's the precious little time we have to accomplish anything that causes us to feel pressure. Deadlines. Some of us are putting in a forty-hour week every day. If we've said it once, we've said it a thousand times: "If only I had more hours in the day." As sincere as that sounds when we say it, we'd probably kill ourselves with more hours in the day—or days in the week—or weeks in the year! We'd just fill up whatever we had.

Jesus didn't have much time to accomplish the Father's will. Three years to spread the message of one way, one truth, and one life across the globe. On foot. Without automobiles or Concorde jets. Without television, the printing press, faxes, Web sites, or email. Jesus had so much to do in so little time that His followers must have gone to sleep exhausted many nights. (Think about how the disciples nodded off in the garden of Gethsemane.) Who knows how many mornings they longed to sleep in, take a day off, or call in sick. But they knew they couldn't. Besides, how could you call in sick to the Great Physician?

Jesus solved the time problem by always being focused. So many souls—so little time. He knew what His mission was, and He was able to say no (that's right, it's okay to say no) to those things that would distract Him from it. The hymn writer may have put it best when he wrote, "Work, for the night is coming when man's work is done."

DON'T WORRY, THERE'S ENOUGH WORK FOR EVERYBODY

Jesus felt the stress that comes from being called to do a great task. Yet He delegated. He left the job to His disciples. Now that has a pressure all its own because no one knew them better than Jesus did. He knew their interactions, their gifts, their compatibilities, and their incompatibilities. He knew their passions, their problems, and their personalities. He knew that they suffered from the human frailties of jealousy, critical spirits, and fragile egos. But He also knew that the cross lay ahead for Him, and it was time to let them take the gospel to the four corners of the earth. Though He promised that He would never leave them alone, He knew He would have to leave them *in charge*. Now that's stress!

If you have kids, can you remember the first time you left one of your children in charge? Once, my wife, Linda, and I left our two sons, Seth and Adam (nineteen and fifteen, respectively), home alone while we visited friends in New York.

From the moment we walked out of the door until the moment we walked back through it three days later, Linda worried. On the whole trip to New York and the entire trip home, we shared many a conversation about all the things that could go wrong. Had I included the list here, this book would have to be a trilogy. We were able to think of so many scenarios because we had heard horror stories from other parents.

The words that kept ringing in our ears were those of our mutual friends, Talmadge and Genell Johnson. They had told us about leaving their sons, Michael and Jeffrey (about the same ages as our boys), alone for the first time, and how Jeffrey, the younger one, decided he'd take the family car out for a drive ... right through the garage door and out the other side!

Another story that remained in my mind came from my long-time tennis partner, Jim Wilcox. He loves to tell about the time he and his brother were left alone for a month one summer while his parents went to Europe. Now these boys were college-age, so it seemed like they would be all right. But little did their parents realize how unprepared Jim and John were for that kind of freedom.

Mom and Dad Wilcox had left the boys with instructions to paint the house while they were away. On day one of their "vacation," the boys got out the rollers and in six-foot letters on the front of the house they painted, "For a good time, call 377-3675." And they left that message up until the day before their parents arrived home. But that wasn't all. One night during that unchaperoned month, a friend of theirs accidently left the freezer door ajar, and by the time it was discovered the next day, an entire side of beef, recently purchased and packed, had thawed out. What did Jim and John do? Why, they hosted the biggest neighborhood barbecue that part of California had ever seen!

JESUS ALSO HAD A JIM AND JOHN

Jesus must have felt the same way as the Wilcox parents did—after all, He too had a Jim and John. And He left them in charge along with Pete, Andy, and the rest of the crew. Jesus left the most important job in the history of mankind to His disciples.

We all know how hard it is to let go of something we've held onto, clutching it closely and caring for it passionately. It's difficult to turn over something we love. And it's sometimes tough to empower less experienced people to do what they need to learn to do. But the marvelous way Jesus handled that stress should be a model for us. He paused, looked toward heaven, and surrendered His will to that of His Father.

Likewise, we must turn over our pressures and our stresses to the Father. We must understand our mission in life—to love God, to love each other, and to glorify God through excellence.

ME WORRY? I'M TOO BUSY FRETTING (OR, DIDN'T I USED TO HAVE FINGERNAILS?)

As if the normal stresses of life aren't enough, we often find worries and anxieties to tote with us from place to place—and then we wonder how they sap our resources and drag us to the bottom!

Hypochondriacs worry constantly about their health or lack of it. If *60 Minutes* covers cancer of the hair follicle, a hypochondriac will believe he's got it—even if he doesn't have much hair left. Each month when he receives his medical journal, he's convinced that he has not only the "Disease of the Month," but also the ones featured on pages twelve, thirty-six, and fifty-one—and on the insert card as well. And they're *all* terminal. Remember the words of Mark

Twain: "Be careful about reading health books. You may die of a misprint."

Homebodies often worry about their house's electricity, plumbing, or foundation. To them, a hairline crack in the wall means a million-dollar repair bill. A drip in the bathroom sends them off to the Yellow Pages for Noah the Plumber's twenty-four-hour emergency line. A repair truck anywhere in the neighborhood is a reason for instant panic. Every noise at night is the coming Apocalypse!

There Is a Cure!

The secret to dealing with stress is to study two words that derive from it: *eustress* and *distress*. Eustress is *good* stress—what Dr. Hans Selye, founder of the Institute of Stress, said is constructive and healthy. It is the type of stress that causes us to grow, to use our internal strength, to show integrity of spirit and resolve of character. At the base of eustress is the conviction that God is with us.

At the end of His great Sermon on the Mount, Jesus said that God's will for us is much less about career choices, family matters, or personal goals than we think; God simply wants us to build our lives on His firm foundation so that when the storms assail us, when the stresses of everyday life overwhelm us, we will not crumble, stumble, or fumble. In other words, God is less concerned about how we buy the bricks of our home than He is with what we anchor those bricks to. It is only when we have built our lives on Him that we will see stress as a challenging opportunity rather than as a source of defeat.

Blessed is the man who perseveres under trial, because when he has stood the test, he will receive the crown of life that God has promised to those who love him. (James 1:12)

Embracing eustress is one thing, but the greater difficulty most of us face is dealing with distress. Some years ago my lifelong friend John C. Maxwell preached at my church. I'll never forget his message: "Don't Let Stress Become Distress." In it, he offered three antidotes to stress. The first is to refocus your thinking. He based it on Paul's admonition in Philippians 4:8: "Whatever is true, whatever is noble, whatever is right, whatever is pure, whatever is lovely, whatever is admirable—if anything is excellent or praiseworthy—think about such things."

"To deal with stressful feelings," John said, "we need to change both our perspective and our expectations. This helps us see circumstances the way God sees them. And He is more concerned with serving the needs of others than with meeting our human expectations."

Second, John said we must "release the pressure." Let's face it: We are more like pressure cookers than we are teakettles. When a teakettle begins to boil, it just whistles. Few of us have mastered that skill. Most people let things get to a boiling point, still holding down the lid with all their strength, until there's an explosion that affects everything and everyone around them. Not a very healthy or beneficial situation for anyone.

One of the best outlets for stress is having fun. How would you like your doctor to write that on your prescription? But the medical profession does indeed admit that leisure time and fun are a part of a healthy regimen. Think about it. When's the last time you saw

Mickey Mouse in therapy? As we spend time doing the things we enjoy, some of the pressure we feel can't help but escape. We can unwind and focus on activities that take our minds off of our worries and help us see life in a better light.

Another thing we should do periodically is list our top priorities. What is *really* important?

> The job?
> The paycheck?
> The bills?
> The children?
> Your spouse?
> Your reputation?
> Your walk with God?

Stress seems to dwindle when we put our microscopes away for awhile and get out telescopes. They enable us to look at the big picture, the long view.

When you are searching to define your priorities, here's a simple exercise you can use. Spend the first half of any weekday watching and listening to elderly people. What do they find important? With what activities do they fill their day? What can they teach us about the value of the ordinary? Then spend the second half of the day watching small children. What's important to them? What are their major concerns? Nineteenth-century British poet William Wordsworth called the child the "best philosopher … Mighty Prophet! Seer blest!" and "the Father of Man." He had obviously watched children play and knew they held the secret to immortality.

Now, are *you* still wondering who signed you up for the whole day? Why not set aside some time to regain your perspective? You just might see the day's stress in a whole new light.

CHAPTER 3

I've Discovered the Answers to Life and Death—

Now If I Could Just Figure Out

All That Stuff in Between

One dark night on a youth group campout in the nearby mountains, the kids of Springdale Church decided to go for a midnight hike. (That's a funny thing about teens—at home they won't even walk next door. And they would never be caught dead walking to school. But offer them a hot tent as an option, and they'll walk for miles.)

After an hour or so of hiking in the pitch black, a boy named Kenny strayed from the group and ended up lost. While attempting to find his way back to his friends, he slipped down the face of a rock, certain that he would plummet to his death. In desperation, he grabbed the one-inch trunk of a small tree growing out of the rock face and held on with all his might.

"Help!" he screamed. "Somebody help me!"

Just as the rest of the group was returning back to their campsite, Tim, the youth director, heard the cries, and the whole posse ran toward the noise. Never a hearty boy by nature, Kenny was beginning to lose his strength, and his screams were becoming frantic. He knew that if Tim and others didn't reach him soon, he would fall some two hundred feet to his ... well, he didn't even want to think about that.

"We're coming!" Tim called out. "Hold on!"

"Hurry!" Kenny shouted. "I'm about to let go."

Kenny was miserable about his predicament. He worried about the fall, about how his parents would react to the news of his ... well, he still didn't want to think about that. Knowing he had only seconds before exhaustion would surely overcome him, he gathered up all his strength and cried out one last time, "I can't hold on! I'm slipping! Heeellllpppp!"

Tim had barely descended the mountainside some fifty feet when Kenny let out a horrible death scream. And he fell.

Fortunately, Kenny's *six-inch fall* was interrupted abruptly by a *five-foot-wide path* that led directly back to the campsite!

Sometimes we worry and fight and struggle until we reach utter exhaustion over what turns out to be nothing more than the smallest of inconveniences. All we really need to do is to let go and fall helplessly into the open arms of God.

STAY OUT OF A RUT, EVEN WHEN YOU'RE IN THE TRENCHES

A French soldier in World War I used to carry a little card with him to help him overcome worry.

> Of two things, one is certain. Either you are at the front,
> or you are behind the lines. If you are at the front, of two
> things, one is certain. Either you are exposed to danger,
> or you are in a safe place. If you are exposed to danger,

of two things, one is certain. Either you are wounded, or you are not wounded. If you are wounded, of two things, one is certain. Either you recover, or you die. If you recover, there is no need to worry. If you die, you cannot worry. SO WHY WORRY.[6]

The *Washington Post* conducted a survey in 1996 asking its readers what worried them the most. Of the eighty possible worries listed in the questionnaire, the issues that caused the most concern were the educational system, crime, AIDS, welfare, drug use, illegal immigration, and the cost of medical care.

Now those are certainly some national and global concerns to be reckoned with and reconciled, but many of them seem almost too big to worry about, don't they? Deep down, we know that we can't do much as individuals to relieve any of them. So we instead tend to fill our minds with other worries that come a bit closer to home:

- the boss at work
- the kids
- the kids' friends
- the bills on the kitchen table
- the bills on the bedroom dresser
- the bills left in the mailbox in hopes that they'll go away, etc.

Yet even most of these worries are unnecessary. According to most psychological statistics regarding worry, 40 percent of our worries never come to pass. Thirty percent involve past decisions that cannot be changed. Twelve percent of our worries focus on criticism from others who spoke simply because they felt inferior. Ten percent center on our health, which just gets worse when we worry. (You know what they say anyway, don't you? Being in the best of health merely means you're dying at a slower pace.) And finally, only 8 percent of our worries can actually be described as "legitimate" causes for our attention. In other words, if we weren't so busy wasting time on all those problems that will never come to pass, we'd have a little more time and energy to handle the mere 8 percent that will happen.

THIS IS NOTHING THAT FIVE YEARS CAN'T SOLVE

To get a handle on what *really* matters, think about what Leonard Thomas says: "If you want to test your memory, try to remember what you were worrying about a year ago." What a profound statement. Try to list five things you were fretting about last year. And if you can indeed come up with five, write down the outcome of those five situations. Did you have much real control over what occurred?

Five years ago, if you were worrying about losing your hair, by now you either still have it or it's sitting on your dresser. Worrying about it didn't help matters a bit.

Five years ago, you might have worried that you wouldn't have enough money to pay your bills. I would venture to guess that by now you're either still paying those same bills or you've added others to take their place. (Maybe both!) Worrying about them didn't lower your outstanding balance one penny.

Five years ago, you might have worried about your child marrying a girl or boy not of your choosing. Now, here you are five years later, and your child is dating someone else who makes the original "bad" choice look like Prince or Princess Charming.

So now, don't you wonder why you wasted so much time worrying? I once read in *Decision* magazine, "You can't change the past, but you can ruin a perfectly good present by worrying about the future." That's so true. Planning for tomorrow is perfectly all right. Worrying over it, fretting about it, or losing sleep because of it isn't. Stationery stores sell day planners, month planners, and year planners. They don't sell "day worry charts," "month worry charts," or "year worry charts." If we all turned off our beepers, our cell phones, and our laptops, would the world come to an end? No, but it would get a whole lot quieter!

Rewrite Your Calendar

Too many of us want it both ways. If our calendars are filled with appointments, dates, meetings, and commitments, we complain that we're never going to meet all those responsibilities, along with the many additional duties that aren't even listed. Conversely, if our calendars are empty, we worry that nobody likes us, trusts, us, or needs us. Then we fall into the trap of self-pity and, eventually, depression.

What if we began filling our calendars with a different set of priorities? What if we matched every "meet client for business lunch at Zorba's," with an entry that said "meet Joey at the school cafeteria for pizza day"? Not only would Joey appreciate it, but God would too. After all, eating school cafeteria food displays *tremendous faith*.

And what if we changed the calendar entry "Company weekend seminar in Detroit" to "Family weekend at the lake"? After all, which would you *really* rather be doing—be in a dull meeting with a room full of jet-setters or be with your kids jet skiing? No doubt things in this country would change if we scheduled as much time for TLC as we do for GNP.

So where does worry fit into the lifestyle of the Christian? Here's what Peter Alwinson had to say in his article "Antsy Spirituality: Relief for the Worried":

> The point is not that Christians will ever stop worrying. The point is that we get to the place where our worry doesn't control us. At that place, we learn to utilize the faith that God has given us to take us out of the pit of worry and into the light of faith.

WHAT DOES JESUS SAY ABOUT WORRY?

In His great sermon, Jesus said,

> *Therefore I tell you, do not worry about your life, what you will eat or drink; or about your body, what you will wear. Is not life more important than food, and the body more important than clothes? Look at the birds of the air; they do not sow or reap or store away in barns, and yet your heavenly Father feeds them. Are you not much more valuable than they? Who of you by worrying can add a single hour to his life? (Matt. 6:25–27)*

Now, I don't know if there was a Jerusalem outlet mall, but Jesus even covered the topic of clothing as well. He went on to say:

And why do you worry about clothes? See how the lilies of the field grow. They do not labor or spin. Yet I tell you that not even Solomon in all his splendor was dressed like one of these. If that is how God clothes the grass of the field, which is here today and tomorrow is thrown in the fire, will he not much more clothe you, O you of little faith? So do not worry, saying, "What shall we eat?" or "What shall we drink?" or "What shall we wear?" For the pagans run after all these things, and your heavenly Father knows that you need them. But seek first his kingdom and his righteousness, and all these things will be given to you as well. Therefore do not worry about tomorrow, for tomorrow will worry about itself. Each day has enough trouble of its own. (Matt. 6:28–34)

I believe that as Jesus continued teaching, He studied His listeners and saw something. He saw fear. He had just finished talking about treasures on earth and treasures in heaven, and this whole idea of reorienting life around things of eternal value … and, well, quite frankly, it scared the crowd. Whenever I preach about turning our agenda loose and letting God have His way, what I see on the faces of the people most often is not boredom, defiance, rebellion, or arrogance. Like Jesus, I, too, see fear.

You've Got to Let Go

It's hard to let go and trust God completely. We're afraid if we trust God with our finances and give generously toward His kingdom, we'll end up living in a cardboard box under a freeway on-ramp. We're afraid if we wait on God to bring us the spouse of His choice, we'll end up with Quasimodo (or Quasimodette) on a bad hair day. If we trust His timing with our careers, we'll spend the rest of our lives saying, "You want fries with that?"

Caution helps us avoid legitimate danger, but fear can keep us from enjoying all that God has for us. Not only did Jesus see fear on the people's faces, He saw fear's constant companion: *worry.* So Jesus tried to convey to the crowd, "Snap out of it." I'm paraphrasing a bit, of course, but He did remind them—as He reminds us—that our basic needs are His problem. *He takes care of that which He creates.*

Of all the biblical stories illustrating worry, none is more practical or clear than the one recorded in the last five verses of Luke 10. Jesus had dropped by His friends' home in Bethany. He was, no doubt, tired after a full day, so nothing meant more to Him than having a quiet place to relax with loved ones who understood. However, one of His friends, Martha, turned the occasion into a mild tempest with her frenzied behavior.

In an effort to prepare a huge meal for Jesus, Martha scurried around the kitchen, kneading the dough for bread, boiling the veggies, basting the lamb ... and maybe, just maybe, slamming down a pot or two ... and maybe, just maybe, the dough fell flat ... and maybe, just maybe, the lamb was starting to burn. And that finally pushed her right over the edge! As the veggies started to boil over, so did Martha. Then her frustration turned into blame.

"Lord," she said, "if my sister, Mary, doesn't get in here to help me with this dinner, I'm ordering *take out!*" (Again, I'm paraphrasing just a bit!)

Martha was probably steamed at Mary on two counts. First, she wanted Mary to carry her part of the workload, and second, she wanted Mary to carry her part of the *worry* load. Perhaps you know someone like Martha, who views worry as a team sport. It's not enough for one person to worry. She wants you to be chewing your share of fingernails too. If you'd pace your half of the floor, it'd make his pacing that much easier. But notice the careful reply of our Lord:

> *Martha, Martha ... you are worried and upset about many things, but only one thing is needed. Mary has chosen what is better, and it will not be taken away from her. (Luke 10:41–42)*

Jesus used the word *worry* to describe Martha's attitude. She had a divided mind—Jesus, work, Jesus, chores, Jesus, dinner. Contrast that with the picture of her sister, Mary, who was single-minded. She just wanted to spend time with *Jesus.*

PERMISSION TO WORRY

So, what is wrong with worry? It's incompatible with faith. The two simply do not mix. But if you truly *enjoy* worrying, if it's so much a part of you that you can't give it up without a twelve-step program or a "worry patch" applied to your arm, then consider this: Jesus has given you the "green light" to worry in certain circumstances. First, you have His permission to worry *when it will feed and clothe you.* In other words, when you can eat an anxiety attack or wear an ulcer, then worry's all right with Him. The only problem is that you can't eat worry, but it can eat you. If that weren't true, why would Tagamet, an antiulcer medicine, be posting recent sales of well over $800 million?

We can learn a lot from animals, you know. Have you ever seen a bird try to build and live in two, three, maybe even four nests, each with its own mortgage? Or have you ever heard of a fox that had to see the animal psychologist because of a problem with low self-esteem? I've yet to see an episode of *Rescue 911* devoted to a cat who was stressing out because he was down to his last three lives or to a squirrel who tried to gather two winters' worth of nuts and suffered an attack of angina in the process.

Secondly, Jesus gives us permission to worry when it will make us live longer and grow taller. If worry added height to our stature, we wouldn't need high heels. If it added years to our lives, we wouldn't need doctors. The fact of the matter is, it doesn't do either of those things—it does just the opposite. Stress takes years from our lives, and worry hunches our shoulders and lowers our heads.

There was a front-page story in *The Daily Oklahoman* about the correlation between emotional stress and heart attacks. In the story, Duke University specialist James Blumenthal said, "If you demonstrate abnormal heart function in response to mental stress, your increased risk for suffering a future cardiac event is two-to-threefold."

Thirdly, you have our Lord's permission to worry when you want to know how a pagan feels. The word *pagan,* in fact, has two possible meanings: a person without a god, or a person without a *reliable* god. Jesus said that if you want to know how that feels, then worry. After all, worry is nothing more than unfaith. It is the suspicion that we do not really have a loving Father who's fighting along with us. It is a symptom of an absentee god—something we as Christians do not have.

It is said that in the late 1930s, as the Nazis were moving through the Netherlands, a group of Christians came to a theologian by the name of Henry Kramer and said, "Our Jewish neighbors are disappearing in the night. What should we do?" Kramer responded, "I cannot tell you what to do … I can only tell you who you are." Christians must always strive to be like their Master.

In the passage from Luke, Jesus was saying that those who are citizens in His kingdom will be cared for. If they seek Him first, He does not have a bad memory—He will not forget who they are.

Lastly, we have Jesus' permission to worry when we want tomorrow to be worse than it's already going to be. So much for our classic relief phrase, "Don't worry. Everything will turn out okay." Jesus blew that one to smithereens! He said, in so many words, "Don't worry. Everything's *not* going to be okay. In fact, tomorrow is going to bring its own share of troubles." But worrying about them ahead of time only throws more bricks on today's wagon, and it's already loaded. As Peter Marshall, late chaplain of the United States Senate, once said, "God, help us to do our very best this day and be content with today's troubles, so that we shall not borrow the troubles of tomorrow." Take each day with its blessings and testings as they come. God has not cut us adrift in this world. He's in the boat with us. He cares enough about us to be with us in every tomorrow.

No matter how you slice it, you can't find a good reason to worry. We can't even find a legitimate excuse in saying we care about what's important to God. As Oswald Chambers once said, "The great concern of our lives is not the kingdom of God, but how we are going to take care of ourselves to live. Jesus reversed the order by telling us to get the right relationship with God first, maintaining it as the primary concern of our lives, and never to place our concern on taking care of the other things of life."[7] That's good advice.

Worry Is the Imagination Run Amok

Someone has said, "Worry is simply the misuse of God's creative imagination which He has placed within each of us." Peter Alwinson takes this one step further. He says, "When we worry, we're taking the imaginative abilities that God has given us and we work them way out of proportion. We've abused them. Worry is simply imagination gone awry."

In his book *The Cycle of Victorious Living,* author Earl Lee said,

> Tension is normal and natural in life. Without tension we could not exist any more than a violin string can be played without being stretched across the bridge. The creative tension is not the same thing as destructive worry. Worry is like racing an automobile engine while it's in neutral. The gas and noise and smog do not get us anywhere. But legitimate concern (creative tension) is putting the car into low gear on your way to moving ahead. You tell yourself that you are going to use the power God has given you to do something about the situation which could cause you to fret. One really moved into high gear when he affirms, "Now unto him that is able to do exceeding abundantly above all that we ask or think, according to the power that worketh in us, unto him be glory." That scripture goes places, and you go with it. It's a long way from worrying, fretting,

and stewing in a state of paralysis.... Fret, usually, is not removed by praying but by doing.

Lee went on to dismantle the disclaimer offered by so many: "Oh, I'm just a worrywart." He said that if we examine the worrywart, we will find that his malady is malignant.

> It eats down into the spirit until it destroys life. The only way to handle this critical malignancy is to let the Holy Spirit operate on it—because FRET TAKES US OUT OF ORBIT. It is the cell malfunctioning, refusing to work with the normal, happily functioning body cells. It has become self-centered and its refusal to cooperate can bring death. It takes a specialist to handle a malignancy, and the Holy Spirit is the Great Specialist. But He can operate only on the yielded spirit, and the anesthetic is grace.[8]

A Bridge Too Soon

Have you ever heard the adage "We'll cross that bridge when we get to it"? It is a paraphrase of something the companions of Abraham Lincoln were told when they were heading to his first presidential inauguration as the nation stood on the precipice of civil war. As they neared the swollen Fox River, one of his colleagues asked, "If these streams give us so much trouble, how shall we get over Fox River?" At a log tavern where they stopped as night fell, they met a man quite familiar with the peculiarities of the area and its terrain. They asked him about the Fox River.

"Oh, yes," replied the circuit rider, "I know all about the Fox River. I have crossed it often and understand it well. But I have one fixed rule with regard to Fox River—I never cross it till I reach it."[9]

God has a habit of coming to our aid *when* we need it. Think about it. God didn't part the Red Sea until Moses got up to its banks, either. That's when Moses *needed* it parted. Not five miles back. Not ten miles back. Moses didn't need it parted until he and the Israelites were ready to step into the water. When that moment came, God was there with a way of escape.

Sir Thomas Carlyle, the famous British essayist, once built a soundproof chamber in his house to block out all the noise around him so that he could work. Obviously, Carlyle was easily distracted, so when a new neighbor moved in with a rooster that crowed at night, Carlyle was quite upset.

"But he crows only three times a night," he was told. "Surely that can't be that much of an annoyance."

But Carlyle replied, "If you only knew what I suffer just waiting for that cock to crow!"

We get so concerned with what *might* happen—anticipating the worst in every possible situation—that the joy in our lives is stifled by fruitless fretting. We spend so much time waiting for the "other shoe to drop" that we miss the enjoyment and peace of the silence. W. Phillip Keller said it this way:

> *We fret and fume and fuss about the unknown future.*
> *We drag tomorrow's imagined difficulties into this day.*
> *So we desecrate each day with stress and strain.*
> *Our Father never intended us to live that way.*

He gives us life one day at a time.
Yesterday is gone.
Only today is mine to relish at a gentle pace.
It is too precious to overload.
So it is to be enjoyed in serenity and strength,
Put first things first.
The petty distractions can wait.
Time erases most of them.[10]

A great way to get your mind off your problems is to exercise. Walk, jog, bench press your bills—do anything as long as it takes energy. It's been medically proven that physical exercise is a great natural antidepressant (just don't do it in Spandex shorts in front of a mirror).

There's a wonderful verse that should be on every Christian's mirror so they can read it first thing every morning and last thing every night. Its imperatives offer simplistic yet profound methods for dealing with the worries of life. It's titled "Promise Yourself," by Christian D. Larson. It says *promise yourself*…

To be so strong that nothing can disturb your peace of mind.

To talk health, happiness, and prosperity to every person you meet.

To make all your friends feel that there is something in them.

To look at the sunny side of everything and make your optimism come true.

To think only of the best, to work only for the best, and to expect only the best.

To be just as enthusiastic about the success of others as you are about your own.

To forget the mistakes of the past and press on to the greater achievements of the future.

To wear a cheerful countenance at all times and give every living creature you meet a smile.

To give so much time to the improvement of yourself that you have no time to criticize others.

To be too large for worry, too noble for anger, too strong for fear, and too happy to permit the presence of trouble.

There's nothing that cheers the soul like a positive promise made—and kept—to yourself. Isn't it about time you made some promises to yourself?

CHAPTER 4

Hey, Who Stuck That Fork in My Road?

During World War II, when many of the able-bodied of the nation were overseas, the owner of a small apple orchard decided to employ a group of boys to pick his crop. A few of the boys seemed to eat as many as they picked or throw them at the other boys, but there were many good workers who did more than their share.

Out of that best group of boys, the man decided that he would pick someone to be his sorter, and since a boy named Jimmy seemed to work at a faster pace than any of the rest, he got the job. The old farmer sat him at a table with three large baskets and told him to sort all of the apples into small, medium, and large. And since he knew the boy was a good worker, the man went off to town to buy some supplies.

When he got back, he saw poor Jimmy sitting behind a mountain of fruit, with one apple in each of his hands and puzzled look on his face.

"What in the world happened?" said the orchard owner.

"All these apples look the same to me," the boy said with a puzzled look on his face. "I can pick 'em, but I guess I just can't choose 'em."

FORKS, S CURVES, AND U-TURNS

Do you feel the same way about making decisions? Maybe you even find it hard to follow the advice given by Yogi Berra: "If you come to a fork in the road, take it." If that sounds like you, you're not alone. In looking back over your life, you will see that there are many occasions when the journey gave you two difficult options. There have also been times when it took a sharp turn to the left or the right.

Changing course can be a primary agent of stress. Some people might suggest that redirection is good and healthy—a sort of evolutionary process—while others will testify to severe clinical depression when confronted with abrupt and profound interruptions in their routines.

I have a friend named Jim. He and I are like night and day when it comes to these forks in the road. I love challenges. I enjoy travel, I purchase every new tennis racket that comes out (almost!), and I've probably eaten in 459 different restaurants this year. In fact, I get bummed out if something big doesn't alter the direction in my life (just a little bit) every couple of months. Jim, on the other hand, breaks out into a cold sweat each time he is confronted with one too many options. (Sometimes one option seems like one too many for him!)

When Jim goes to Baskin-Robbins, he'll stand at the counter trying to make up his mind until closing time. He hates making decisions, and he hates change. He'll drive a car until he sees its parts in the rearview mirror. He still plays baseball with his childhood glove. Every time he moves, he claims that the next move he makes will be in a pine box. Does he plan a vacation? Forget it. A vacation for Jim is when *everybody else* leaves town.

Jim is a great guy, but he always wants to walk to the same restaurant just two or three blocks away, get the same waitress, order the same food, and pay what he paid two decades ago. (And believe me, that waitress is never very thrilled with that quarter tip he leaves, either!)

GO KNOCK SOMEWHERE ELSE

Some people don't seem to recognize the opportunity for positive change, even when it comes up and bites them. Maxie Dunnam of Asbury Seminary tells a story about an elderly man who began spending a significant amount of time with an elderly woman. Neither had ever married and each had lived alone for many years. Gradually, the old gentleman recognized real attachment to her but was very shy and afraid to reveal his feelings to her. After many days of anxiety and fear, he finally mustered up the courage to declare his intentions. He went over to her home and in a nervous frenzy blurted out, "Let's get married!"

Surprised, the woman threw her hands in the air and shouted, "What a wonderful idea, but who in the world would have us?"

There's just no way around it. Decisions often cause people stress. Look at chronic dieters, for example. Ask them to make a decision about their diets, and they'll go over the edge. Recently I read about something called "The Stress Diet." It's a perfect match for the habitually tense dieter:

> Breakfast: half a grapefruit, one slice whole wheat toast,
> eight ounces skim milk.

Lunch: four ounces lean boiled chicken breast, one cup steamed zucchini, one Oreo cookie, herb tea.

Mid-afternoon Snack: Rest of the package of Oreos, one quart rocky road ice cream, one jar hot fudge.

Dinner: two loaves garlic bread, a large cheese and mushroom pizza, large pitcher of root beer, two Milky Way candy bars, entire Sara Lee cheesecake eaten directly from the refrigerator.

IF YOU STAND AT THE CROSSROADS TOO LONG, YOU'LL GET RUN OVER

No good comes from worrying over decisions. Dr. Charles Mayo observed that "worry affects the circulation, the heart, the glands, the whole nervous system. I have never known a man who died from overwork, but many who died from doubt."

Several years ago, Doctors Holmes and Rahe of the University of Washington performed a study on stress. They found over forty events in life that create a great deal of strain. At the heart of each was this idea of coming to a fork in the road: the death of a spouse, the loss of a job, bankruptcy, divorce, etc. They even found that the positive forks in our journey that we initiate ourselves can be stressful too. Major changes like purchasing a car, changing careers, buying or building a new home, having a baby, or having a baby turn two can be exciting but stressful. But whenever major changes occur involuntarily and suddenly, they cause even more trouble.

MOMENTARY PARALYSIS

Franz Kafka wrote a great short story that poignantly illustrates the internal struggle a person deals with when facing a fork in the road. The story is called "The Bucket Rider." It tells of a man who is freezing to death out in the snow. Approaching a town, he sees one light on in a window and is drawn to it. The light comes from the home of the town's coal dealer and his wife. The half-frozen man knocks on the door, but only the coal dealer hears the man's desperate cries outside. The coal dealer's wife, deaf to the pleas, wants her husband to come away from the door to cool their fire, which has grown too warm. After a while, the coal dealer obeys his wife and leaves the man outside to die.

This tale represents the two voices each of us hears when we are faced with change, conflict, or the need for action. There is a voice that says "yes," while another says "no." A voice that says "do it" and another that says "ignore it." A voice that says "here" but a second that says "there." A voice that says "fight" while the other says "flee." Each time we hear these two voices, we react physically. Our pulse picks up, our adrenal gland starts pumping wildly, our entire body prepares for battle. The coal dealer and his wife in Kafka's story personify this internal dialogue that you and I frequently experience. Every time we see a car broken down on the freeway, we think, "Should I help that guy, or is he an escaped serial killer?" When confronted with a person holding a sign that says, "Will work for food," we ask ourselves, "Does this guy need legitimate help, or is he making more money than I am?" When we see a fellow employee taking things home from the office, our internal debate is, "Should I talk to him, should I talk to the boss, or should I just hope someone else notices that fax machine tucked under his jacket?"

CONFUSION AT THE CROSSROADS

When you're at a crossroads, you deal with one of three common sources of confusion: indecision, imagination, or the inevitable. The first may be the hardest to deal with, but the quickest to be resolved because if we were honest with ourselves, we would admit that life is sometimes little more than decisions and their consequences. The decision of whether to go to a small private college or a large state university can dictate our careers, our mates, our future. The decision to say "I love you" or "I'll see you later" certainly has an obvious impact. The decision to be a doctor or just sell cars to doctors makes a difference in what courses we take in college. And then there's the decision to live a quiet, peaceful life—or have children.

There are even more serious questions we must consider: Am I living for success or significance? Will I invest my life by *giving* all I can or ingest my life by *getting* all I can? Will I accept others as they are or spend my days judging them for what they're not? Will I stand firm in my faith—or fall flat on my face?

The secret to handling the stress of indecision is to jump off the fence and land on one side or the other. In most cases, if we follow our hearts, we'll be making the right decision.

The second source of crossroads confusion is the imagination—a writer's greatest gift but a worrier's biggest curse. The imagination plagues the person who apparently doesn't have enough real stress in his life, so he makes it up. A hangnail becomes an amputation, an unexpected bill a bankruptcy, a flat tire means the car got totaled. Every event in his life is exaggerated beyond recognition, and he spends his whole day waiting for doomsday to occur. His knuckles are raw from knocking on wood, and his journal is filled with more complaints than a DMV How-Can-We-Serve-You-Better suggestion box. His entire self-image is based on his ability to foresee trouble and to put out all the fires before they burn out of control.

I know of someone who sees every stopped-up toilet as an explosion waiting to happen. She once forced five fire trucks to rush to her office on a Sunday afternoon when the toilet she used overflowed and shorted out the fire alarm system. And then there's the man we know who goes out to the freezing cold every night to check his car doors because he has twice had to deal with dead batteries before he could get to work.

The truth of the matter is that 90 percent of all the imagined catastrophes in the world never happen. They simply stay in the mind of the beholder until a new tragedy can take their place.

Life doesn't have to be that way. Recently, I received the following fax from a friend:

Dear Lord,

So far today, God, I've done all right. I haven't gossiped, haven't lost my temper, haven't been greedy, grumpy, nasty, selfish, or overindulgent. I'm really glad about that. But in a few minutes, God, I'm going to get out of bed, and from then on I'm probably going to need a lot more help. Thank You, in Jesus' name. Amen.

What a hoot! And so true to life! Too many times we anticipate the absolute worst scenario for everyday life.

The third source of crossroads confusion is the inevitable. There are certain laws of nature that we can all count on. For example, we will all die. Some of us will have the privilege of aging toward that, but others will die before reaching full maturity. Other laws state that if you play golf in a thunderstorm, you will be struck by lightning before you make it to the PGA. If you starve yourself in order to fit into your wedding dress, you will faint on camera at your wedding and have the entire scene featured on *America's Funniest Home Videos*. And if you hit your younger brother throughout your childhood, he will outgrow you one day, and then *you're going down!* (I can attest to that one personally.)

While I was contemplating the inevitable recently, I reviewed Murphy's Law: Whatever can go wrong will, and at the worst possible time. There are a few inescapable truths that even Murphy didn't know about:

> *If it sounds too good to be true and is destined to turn out not to be true, you just invested in it.*

> *For every win-win situation, there's a third party without a win—that would be you.*

> *If you put your best foot forward, a baby stroller will roll over it.*

> *The best things in life are free, but the ones intended for you will be delivered to the wrong house.*

If you see a shooting star, it'll be in the moments just before it lands on you.

If everything's coming up roses, you're probably at your own funeral.
—Martha Bolton

Bad things do happen to good people. In other words, you probably will experience a hurried dash to the emergency room one night. You may get a speeding ticket on your way home from church ... with one of the deacons driving behind you to witness the whole thing. Air conditioners do break down on the Fourth of July. You will forget an important anniversary. Your husband will give you a major appliance on your birthday—something really romantic like an electric prune pitter. Your wife will burn dinner on the night your folks drop in. Life is full of unexpected disasters no matter how nice a person you are.

Get Out on a Limb

The secret to coping with these inevitabilities is to stop taking yourself so seriously. Learn to laugh at the face in the mirror daily. Sing in the shower (just don't hit the high notes with your mouth under the spout, or you will drown). Spend time on the swings at the park. Fly a kite. Read as much fiction as you do nonfiction. Sleep in one day when you're not supposed to (Sunday mornings excluded). For every shirt you buy, give one away. Beat fate to the punch!

I'm not saying Fred is a hypochondriac, but he did tell
me he wanted his tombstone to read, "See!"

When you come to the end of your days, you don't want to regret not having lived. Author Tony Campolo once interviewed fifty men over ninety years old, and he asked them what they wish they had done more of in life. Their responses fell into these three categories: "I would risk more," "I would reflect more," and "I would leave something that would live on after I am gone." When you're at the end of your road, it's too late to take the fork, so get moving today.

HIS CROSSROADS LED TO THE CROSS

We're not alone when it comes to facing tough decisions. Jesus experienced them too. He was misunderstood and misrepresented, and He was rejected and crucified. For us, it's bad enough to make difficult choices, but it's even tougher when you heap rejection on top of it.

Have you ever felt uncomfortable when trying to get inside a group or family situation where you didn't feel accepted? All of us want people to like us and accept us. We really do care what others think, yet we read in John 1:11 that in the beginning of Jesus' ministry "he came unto his own, and his own received him not" (KJV). His family rejected Him. The religious leaders rejected Him. His family and friends recognized Him only as the carpenter's son. The Jews knew Him only as another teacher. The religious leaders labeled Him yet another in a long series of self-proclaimed messiahs.

"Who is this nut, anyhow," they must have asked, "who teaches that we must face trials and tribulations, but if we follow Him, we will receive eternal life?"

Not only was Jesus misunderstood, misrepresented, and rejected, but He, too, faced temptation. He was tempted by Satan to prove

Himself the Son of God by turning rock to bread and leaping off a mountain. In the end, He was tempted to believe that God had turned His back on Him and left Him there to die a horrible, humiliating death.

Even dying saints face this temptation. As a pastor, I have seen it many times: A woman who has followed God intensely for sixty-four years is taking her last breath and suddenly is tempted to doubt God's promise of heaven because Satan puts a seed of anxiety in her mind. But there is comfort and good counsel for someone like her: "You've served God faithfully for sixty-four years. Your desire has always been to follow Him. Satan cannot rob you of seeing glory right now because God is holding your hand."

Jesus may have been tempted during His final hours on earth. He may have even said, "I don't want to go through with this!" There were undoubtedly a few of His disciples who agreed, saying, "Master, You don't have to go through with this." But Jesus *did*. And facing the temptation of doubt again while on the cross, when things could not seem bleaker and hope could not feel any farther away, He looked heavenward with tears of desperation in His eyes and cried out to His Father, "Why have you forsaken me?" (Matt. 27:46). Praise God that at the very moment, Jesus' spirit fell into the arms of God, to be reunited in body less than forty-eight hours later.

Let's face it: Jesus was given an awesome assignment. When we consider that He bore the burdens of all people for all time and gladly held in His hands the sins of the entire world, we must admit that He is perfectly capable of carrying whatever responsibilities and burdens we happen to have at the moment. And He can guide us safely through any decision we must make.

Perhaps our concern is over the health of a loved one or an assignment at work that's mind-boggling and body wearying. If our to-do lists are coming out each week in hardback, we need to realize that Jesus understands how that feels. He's been there. He identifies with us and says, "Take your cross and follow me.… Come to me, all you who are weary and burdened, and I will give you rest. Take my yoke upon you and learn from me, for I am gentle and humble in heart, and you will find rest for your souls. For my yoke is easy and my burden is light" (see Mark 8:34; Matt. 11:28–30). If we follow Him, He won't lead us astray.

On Your Mark, Get Set, Go!

Once we're ready to follow our Creator, then we're ready to make a move forward. We should begin by looking at ourselves and thinking about who He's created us to be. We must analyze our strengths and weaknesses. When we do what we are good at, we will be able to view our decisions as opportunities and our setbacks as challenges rather than frustrations. Roger Staubach, former quarterback of the Dallas Cowboys, once said, "When I throw [an interception], I can't wait to get my hands on that football. I can't wait to throw another pass." When you know your strengths, you learn from your mistakes.

The next step involves a stress-free process of setting goals and priorities. Paul J. Rosch, MD, president of the American Institute of Stress, has developed a Top Ten List of Ways to Control Stress. It also works well as a kind of preflight checklist before decision making. With all due respect to David Letterman, here is the list:

#10 Allow yourself time out to enjoy personal interests or just to smell the roses.

#9 Don't be afraid to ask questions, solicit suggestions, and share your problems with others.

#8 Make a list of stressful situations in your life.

#7 Divide the list into things you can't avoid or control and things you can hope to influence.

#6 Don't waste your energies in a frustrating attempt to conquer what you can't control.

#5 Use your time and talents effectively to address those stressful situations you can change.

#4 Recognize that some stress is unavoidable— it's part of life.

#3 Learn to say no when asked to do something stressful.

#2 Organize your time in accordance with your priorities.

#1 Set realistic goals and priorities and identify those things you must do first.

If you can step back and approach each fork in the road in a relatively stress-free manner, knowing that you're following Christ and living according to the way God made you, it will make your life a lot simpler. You might even begin to enjoy the turns and twists and forks in the road!

CHAPTER 5

What Problem?

I Went to a Whole Lot of Trouble to Get This Way

I know a man named Jack who becomes almost hysterical whenever something happens to the plumbing in his home. The slightest drip causes him to hyperventilate and shout, "The sky is falling! The sky is falling!" Now, either he has been suppressing some trauma that occurred when he was very young (perhaps his mother saw a plumber's bill during her pregnancy!), or maybe the recall of what happened one Saturday morning over a decade ago is enough to send him over the edge....

Jack had just gotten up and was making his blind way to the kitchen to start some coffee one spring morning several years ago. On the way he ran into his wife, still in her nightgown, who uttered those eleven fateful words, "Do you think you could fix the leak in the bathroom?" (A question that should be used only in the strongest of marriages.)

"Sure thing," he muttered. "I'll be back in a minute."

Without stopping at the coffee maker, Jack (who was still in his Fruit of the Loom briefs) went straight to his tool cabinet and pulled out his plumbing tools: pliers, a flathead screwdriver, and a hammer.

DON'T TRY THIS AT HOME, KIDS ...

When he got to the dripping faucet, he rationalized that if something truly went wrong, he would simply reach in the cabinet under the sink and shut off the water source. Obviously, he had neither read Murphy's Law nor ever fixed a dripping faucet.

He successfully removed the knob on the hot-water faucet and began unscrewing the center of the mechanism underneath. All of a sudden he was standing before Old Faithful in Yellowstone National Park! When the last thread of the screw released its final hold against the hot water behind it, the water pressure shot it toward Jack's left eye at 150 feet per second. Fortunately, he wasn't watching what he was doing, so the screw missed his eye, lodging harmlessly in the ceiling. But the geyser of scalding water that followed was doing major damage to the textured ceiling surface above his head.

Frantically, he looked under the sink. *No shut-off valve!* He searched again. *None. Nada. Nyet, Nein.* That's when he spotted the trash can. He quickly heaved the trash into the hallway, inverted the can, and redirected the geyser into the sink. His wife, Lisa, who had been standing in the doorway, was now wearing last week's garbage as an accent to her nightgown! (A nice look, by the way.)

"What happened?" she asked as innocently and calmly as she could. She had learned through the years of being married to Jack that she could really get under his skin if she acted serene and under control when he was completely hysterical.

"Hold this here," Jack shouted, "while I go get Sam next door. Maybe he knows where the shut-off valve is."

Within a minute, Sam, who had just gone through cancer surgery and was not fully awake himself, came in to seek the elusive valve. *None. Nada. Nyet, Nein.* So he ran down the hall toward the front door to turn off the main valve in the front yard. Unfortunately, he did not see looming ahead the pristine storm door that Lisa had cleaned spotlessly that very morning. And Sam ran right through it, sending thousands of pieces of glass all over the porch, except, of course, for the fifty or sixty small shards that were now embedded in his face, arms, and legs. (A fashion trend that will probably never catch on!)

Meanwhile, Billy—Jack and Lisa's five-year-old, who had just seen a special program about Oklahoma and "those terrible twisters" the night before—knew exactly what he was witnessing. Clad only in his baby briefs, he began circling the living room like a hysterical vulture, screaming at the top of his tiny lungs, *"Tornado! Tornado! Tornado!"*

Finally, after shutting off the main valve, picking all the glass out of Sam's Swiss-cheese skin, and calming Billy down with a nice dose of cough syrup, Jack and Lisa restored order. Eight hours later, they had a new storm door, courtesy of Sam, a newly painted, texture-free ceiling, courtesy of Jack, and a nondrip hot-water faucet, courtesy of a ten-cent rubber washer.

That's why to this very day, whenever Jack sees a plumbing truck in his neighborhood, he can't help but check every faucet in his house to assure himself that each one has a working shut-off valve.

DON'T LOSE HEART

Jack has never been the same since then when it comes to working around the house. Fortunately, he hasn't lost his confidence in other areas. Others aren't so lucky. When I think about people who need a shot in the arm when it comes to confidence, I think of Charlie Brown from the *Peanuts* comic strip, drawn by Charles Schulz. In a recent cartoon I saw poor Charlie talking to his friend Linus about his perpetual feelings of inadequacy.

"You see, Linus," he said, "it goes all the way back to the beginning. The moment I was born and set foot on the stage of life they took one look at me and said, 'Not right for the part.'"

We don't get to choose how we come *into* life, but we do get to choose how we come *out* of it. Bud Wilkinson said, "The man who tried his best and failed is superior to the man who never tried."

U.S. gymnast Cathy Rigby learned that lesson back in 1972 at the Olympics in Munich, Germany. Going into the games, she had one goal—to win a gold medal. She had trained long and hard for it, and she wanted nothing less.

On the day she was scheduled to perform, she prayed for strength and the control to get through her routine without making mistakes. She didn't want to let herself or her country down. She did perform well, but when the competition was over and the winners were announced, she was not among them. She was crushed.

Afterward, she joined her parents in the stands, all set for a good cry. As she sat down, she could barely manage to say, "I'm sorry. I did my best."

"You know that, and I know that," her mother said, "and I'm sure God knows that too." Then her mother said something that

Cathy says she has never forgotten: "Doing your best is more important than being the best." What incredible insight.

I saw an ad in *Time* magazine recently that showed a young man sprinting in a track-and-field event. That in itself wasn't very interesting. What was noteworthy was that he had no feet or hands! A runner, Tony Volpentest races in competitions such as the Paralympics. He has won numerous gold medals, and is the fastest lower-limb amputee in the world, having sprinted one hundred meters in 11.36 seconds. That's faster than most people with two normal legs.

"My goal isn't to run a 9.84 and break Donovan Bailey's [then world] record," says Volpentest, "though I would love to do that. Realistically, my goal as an athlete is to break 11 seconds before I retire. And there's no doubt in my mind I can do that."

Tony Volpentest is a world-class athlete. What's even more remarkable than his ability to run fast without feet is his attitude. He could have spent his young life discouraged, complaining about how his disability has kept him from competing at the highest level. Instead, he just keeps running and getting better.

How Does a Christian Defeat Discouragement?

A writer, telling the story of a visit to Mammoth Cave, Kentucky, recounts how, in a section of the cave known as The Cathedral, the guide mounted a rock called The Pulpit and said he would preach a sermon. It was a short one: "Keep close to your guide," he said. It was very practical advice, for the party soon found that if someone did not keep close to his guide, he could easily get lost in the midst of so many pits, precipices, and defiles.[11]

That same advice is practical for us when we feel discouraged. Often in our hurried and busy lifestyles, the thing we need the most is to get away from the noise, hustle, and bustle in order to better hear the voice of our Master. We need to retreat.

Jesus Himself exemplified this action many times: In order to stay near His Guide, He left the crowds behind and found a quiet place of physical and spiritual rest. His purpose was not simply to escape, but to get a better perspective. Robert Homes said, "It's not so much like hiding in a cave, where you can see nothing, as it is climbing a mountain, where you can see the entire landscape, where you can ask, 'How is everything fitting together and where am I fitting into the scheme?'"[12]

Anytime we lose perspective, an abnormal sense of self-importance and almost indispensability arises within us, and our obsession for control overcomes our willingness to submit to God's control. And it is only when we relinquish control that we are able to take the risks necessary to build the kingdom of God.

In our society, we are indoctrinated to succeed by nearly every influential person we meet and by just about everything around us. Listen to college and university commencement addresses across our nation, and you'll hear a familiar theme: success, leadership, and winning. No one seems to give much attention to the things that usually occur more frequently in life: failure, followership, and losing. The result is that few of us have been taught the value of failing in order to taste success; the lessons that follow can teach us about the ability to rise up from loss.

A New View of Success

Jesus never seemed all that concerned with worldly success. Robert Holmes said,

He tried to get a careful understanding of His mission in life, and He rejected three specific forms of success— fame, wealth, and power. From that point on, He refused to be dismayed by people's disappointment in Him. First, the hierarchy scoffed; then John the Baptist became disillusioned; His own family questioned His choices, and finally even His disciples grew skeptical. Jesus was considered a failure by nearly everyone on earth whose opinion meant a lot to Him.[13]

Too many times we are overly concerned with what others will think of us. When a woman has a baby, infant-clothing stores can barely keep enough "cute things" in stock. If it were left to us fathers, a clean white T-shirt and tiny blue jeans would be fine on our kids for church, shopping, eating, playing, and formal family portraits. (Notice, I didn't mention a diaper change!) But our wives have said it a thousand times (if they've said it once): "The way people think about our children reflects on me as a mother … not you as a father. So, by the power vested in me by our Macy's charge card, he's going to be *cute!*"

A man's symbol of his worth and importance is often his car, the size of his home, even the appearance of his yard. An unkempt yard can have an adverse effect on a man's public image, especially if the grass is so high that three mailmen have disappeared in it in the past six months. It also makes it difficult for the man to get his mail.

Jesus never gauged His self-worth through the eyes of His critics or even His friends. *He knew who He was.* He was never motivated by the public's expectations of what He should or should not do. His focus was on the mission given to Him by His heavenly Father, and He spent His life trying to show us the same thing. But we get caught up comparing ourselves to the Joneses instead of to Jesus. We want the little bit they have instead of the cattle on a thousand hills that our Lord has. We want to be just like them instead of striving to be just like Christ. We don't stop to think that maybe the Joneses have a bigger home, maybe they have a bigger car, but maybe they have a bigger ulcer, too.

Lloyd Ogilvie suggested that a good way to overcome this worry about what the Joneses have or what the Joneses think is to step back and laugh at how ridiculous we appear. There's an old saying that "a good laugh is sunshine in the house." Laughter can change our attitude and lead to a crucial commitment. Ogilvie said,

> To start, we probably need to bring our wants closer to our needs and then we can pray about them more honestly. And a good motive for that is to be able to have more to share with others in real need and with kingdom causes committed to introducing people to the Savior. Furthermore, we can never be free from worry, stress, depression until the day we commit all we are, have, need, want now and forever into His hands.[14]

Until we can live in the same way that we tell others to live—in the care and wisdom of God—we will never be able to let go and let God, to have confidence in ourselves based on our confidence in Him. "Worrisome care," Ogilvie said, "comes from thinking we have to handle life on our own, with our inadequate human resources.

That kind of anxiety is living horizontally, flat out, depending on our own potential. Once we begin to see the humor in our attitudes in those areas Jesus has exposed, we can begin to laugh at ourselves in much more of our daily life. People who can laugh at themselves are fun to be with. Their freedom is contagious."[15]

So how do we get our minds off our own inadequacies? By trusting God. And by helping other people forget their problems. It's amazing how much you start appreciating your own condition when you listen to someone else's troubles for awhile. Visiting terminally ill people in the hospital, taking toys to a shelter, helping feed the homeless, or spending time with people in a nursing home are sure cures for self-doubt and depression—and you won't even need a prescription!

KNOW THAT YOU ARE LOVED

God truly does want the best for us. And He loves us despite our flaws. If we could just see ourselves through His eyes for a moment, it would change our entire perspective.

I have a friend named Ellis who worked for a produce company in California. He was a fine employee, but he was consistently overlooked when it came time for a promotion. Ellis could weld, drive a truck, sort produce, and do just about anything that needed to be done.

One day the manager called Ellis and said, "Ellis, I've got a problem. There's a load of produce sitting on a dock in San Diego, and I don't have anyone to go pick it up." Ellis assured the manager he would drive down and get it. And he did ... in record time. The manager was so impressed that he called Ellis into his office.

"Ellis," he said, "you know we have a salesman's position open right now. How much will it take to get you to take it?" At the time, Ellis was making three hundred dollars a week, so he thought for a moment.

"Four hundred dollars a week," he said.

"It's a deal," the manager said.

That evening as Ellis was clocking out, the manager asked him to step into his office. "Ellis," he said, "you know when you told me you would need only four hundred dollars a week to take the salesman position." Ellis nodded. "Ellis, I was willing to pay you eight hundred dollars a week because if I need someone to weld, you can weld. If I need someone to drive, you can drive. If I need someone to sort, you can sort." Because Ellis underestimated his worth to the company, Ellis missed out on a tremendous blessing. We often do the same thing and limit God's blessings in our lives.

Our heavenly Father has done all He can to express to us how much He cares for His children. Our ability to overcome worry depends a little on us and a lot on God. You see, when we trust God, we rely on *His* character. Is He good? Is He just? Is He fair? Is He reliable? Is He faithful? If He is—and I believe He is—we can trust all the concerns of life to Him ... not only what we need, but who we are.

CHAPTER 6

Are You Undesirable, Unmentionable, or Totally Undone?

Here is a trustworthy saying that deserves full acceptance:
Christ Jesus came into the world to save sinners. (1 Tim. 1:15)

Some of the events that have happened in our lives shape us forever—for good or bad. On April 19, 1995, at 9:02 a.m., something happened that changed lives all over our country. A bomb flattened the Alfred P. Murrah Federal Building in downtown Oklahoma City, Oklahoma.

Word traveled fast through the city and out the few miles to Bethany, the suburban town where I live. Later, friends from California told me that they couldn't believe there had been that kind of terrorist attack on American soil—sentiments later echoed by people across the nation after the 9/11 terrorist attacks. But the Oklahoma City bombing was the first of its kind. Imagine our shock that it could happen in our state. In our town. To people we knew personally. As firefighters and rescue workers traveled to the bomb site to courageously dig out survivors, every pastor in town mobilized to comfort and support the shaken people.

Messages of hope were preached all over Oklahoma in the days following that tragedy. Suddenly people understood the destructive power of a bomb. But they needed to understand the hope and power of God's incredible grace as well. They needed to know that ...

> A bomb cannot cripple love.
>
> A bomb cannot smother faith.
>
> A bomb cannot eradicate courage.
>
> A bomb cannot annihilate memories.
>
> A bomb cannot shatter compassion.
>
> A bomb cannot destroy hope.
>
> A bomb cannot lessen the power of the
> resurrection.

No matter what the circumstances, God's grace is sufficient.

One of my favorite speakers is Florence Littauer. Recently, she and I shared speaking duties at an INJOY conference in Atlanta, Georgia. And as usual, Florence was winning the crowd with her great sense of humor and anecdotes about everyday life. And she spoke about God's grace.

She told one delightful story about a speaking engagement during which she apparently was focusing on the sinfulness of mankind and the need we all have for God's grace. Spontaneously during the speech, Florence asked, "Does anyone here know what *grace* means?"

A seven-year-old girl on the front row, all decked out in a white dress, stood up and raised her hand. "I know, Miss Littauer, I know," she said. "Grace is unmerited favor from God!"

Florence couldn't believe what she had just heard. She then asked the young girl to step up to the platform with her.

"Great answer," Florence said, "now tell the audience what that means."

The little girl folded her hands and shrugged. "I don't have a clue!"

I laugh about that incident every time I think about it, yet I am concerned about those who truly don't have a clue about God's grace and what it means. Mark Twain once said, "Heaven goes by favor. If it went by merit, you would stay out and your dog would go in."

In 2 Corinthians 6:1–2, Paul said, "As God's fellow workers we urge you not to receive God's grace in vain. For he says, 'In the time of my favor I heard you, and in the day of salvation I helped you.' I tell you, now is the time of God's favor, now is the day of salvation."

These words rolled through my mind recently as I pulled my rental car onto Billy Graham Parkway in Charlotte, North Carolina. How often I have heard Billy Graham say, "This is your hour of decision, this is your moment of truth!" And he is so right! We live in the day of God's grace. "For the grace of God that brings salvation has appeared to all men" (Titus 2:11). We live in a time of God's favor.

Like the little girl in Florence's story, maybe you aren't exactly sure what grace is. If that's the case, now is a great time to learn about it and how it is sufficient for you and me regardless of what we are facing.

GRACE IS GOD SUPPLYING OUR NEEDS

Grace is not just a prayer we offer before meals. Nor is it just the name of a person that we have met along life's way. Grace is God at work in our lives. D. L. Moody once said, "Grace is the act of God supplying our needs from day to day as we have them, found in the atonement of Christ." Jesus shed His blood on Calvary's cruel cross to provide grace sufficient to cover all of our sins.

As a young teen attending the historic Mount of Praise camp meeting in Circleville, Ohio, I heard Dr. T. M. Anderson tell a story about the famed British preacher Charles Spurgeon. Riding home after a hard day's work, Spurgeon was feeling tired and depressed. Suddenly, the promise "My grace is sufficient for you" entered his mind. He thought of the tiny fish who might be afraid lest they drink the river dry, but who hear the reassuring word, "Drink up, little fish, My stream is sufficient for you." Spurgeon also thought of a mountain climber who is afraid he might exhaust all of the thin oxygen in the atmosphere. "Breathe away, young man, and fill your lungs," God says, "for My atmosphere is sufficient for you." Spurgeon said that for the first time, he "experienced the joy that Abraham felt when he rejoiced in God's provision."

> *God has not promised to give us all the answers,*
> *but He has promised Grace!*[16]
> —Barbara Johnson

Not only has God promised us His grace, but He is faithful in delivering it on time. At a Billy Graham crusade, the late Corrie ten Boom told the story of how as a child she went to her father and said, "Papa, I don't think I have the faith to handle real trouble. I don't know what I'd do if you should die. I don't think I have the faith that some people have to face trouble."

Corrie's father looked at her tenderly and said, "Corrie, dear, when your father says he will send you to the store tomorrow, does he give the money to you today? No, he gives it to you when you are ready to go to the store. And if you are going on a train trip and need money for a ticket, does your father give you the money when we decide you may take the trip? No, he gives it to you when you are at the depot, all ready to buy your ticket. Corrie, God treats us the same way. He doesn't give you faith until you have a need. When you do, He will certainly give it to you."

The title of this book, *God Has Never Failed Me, but He Sure Has Scared Me to Death a Few Times,* became an everyday reality to me when I accepted my first full-time ministerial assignment in 1973. Moving to Tampa, Florida, to become a young church planter with my new bride, Linda, was indeed an exercise in faith! We drove our car from our college campus in Ohio to Florida by faith. And eating lots of Hamburger Helper became a way of life! We simply learned to rely on the grace of God to meet our every need.

I remember on one occasion, I felt led by the Lord to send fifty dollars to the Carters, missionaries to the American Indians in Arizona, even though I wasn't sure why I was supposed to. Linda and I examined our checkbook and found just fifty-four dollars! We sent the fifty dollars anyhow and the next day, I went back to the post office. To my surprise, my college roommate, J. Michael Walters, had sent us a letter and enclosed a love gift of fifty dollars! (Pretty amazing, considering that he was a student at Asbury Seminary.) Naturally, I hurried home to share the good news with Linda. On the way home, I began to sing an old hymn …

'Tis so sweet to trust in Jesus,
Just to take Him at His Word,
Just to rest upon His promise.
Just to know: 'Thus saith the Lord.'
Jesus, Jesus, how I trust Him!
How I've proved Him o'er and o'er!
Jesus, Jesus, precious Jesus!
O for grace to trust Him more![17]
—Louisa M. R. Stead

Obviously, we were satisfied because God had met our need overnight! But the Carters wrote back two weeks later and said, "Your check for fifty dollars arrived just on time. We were preparing to cancel a doctor's appointment for our daughter, Angie, because we didn't have the money." Would you believe, they needed exactly fifty dollars!

In his book *The Applause of Heaven*, Max Lucado gave a magnificent portrait of God. Following his declaration that God does not save us because of what we've done, he added these provocative words: "Only a puny god could be bought with tithes. Only an egotistical god would be impressed with our pain. Only a temperamental god could be satisfied by sacrifices. Only a heartless god would sell salvation to the highest bidders. And only a great god does for His children what they can't do for themselves."

He then added this poignant description of God's grace: "God's delight is received upon surrender, not awarded upon conquest. The first step to joy is a plea for help."[18]

No wonder the apostle Paul said, "But he said to me, 'My grace is sufficient for you, for my power is made perfect in weakness.'

Therefore, I will boast all the more gladly about my weaknesses, so that Christ's power may rest on me. That is why, for Christ's sake, I delight in weaknesses, in insults, in hardships, in persecutions, in difficulties. For when I am weak, then I am strong" (2 Cor. 12:9–10). God hears our plea for help and provides sufficient grace. And He is never late.

GRACE IS GOD CLEANSING US FROM SIN

"For it is by grace you have been saved, through faith—and this not from yourselves, it is the gift of God—not by works, so that no one can boast" (Eph. 2:8–9). What a wonderful passage of Scripture; in fact, almost all evangelical Christians exult in the fact that salvation is by grace through faith and is not based on works or merit on our part. We have turned in faith to Jesus Christ alone for our salvation.

Missionary Milton Cunningham illustrated this truth so wonderfully. Milton was flying on a plane from Atlanta to Dallas and happened to have the middle of the three seats on one side of the aisle. To his right, sitting next to the window, was a young girl who obviously had Down syndrome. She began to ask him some very simple but almost offensive questions.

"Mister," she said to Cunningham, "did you brush your teeth this morning?"

Cunningham, very shocked at the question, squirmed around a bit and then said, "Well, yes, I brushed my teeth this morning."

The young girl said, "Good, 'cause that's what you're supposed to do." Then she asked, "Mister, do you smoke?"

Again, Cunningham was a little uncomfortable, but he told her with a little chuckle that he didn't.

She said, "Good, 'cause smoking will make you die." Then she said, "Mister, do you love Jesus?"

Cunningham was really caught by the simplicity and the forthrightness of the little girl's questions. He smiled and said, "Well, yes, I do love Jesus."

The little girl with Down syndrome smiled and said, "Good, 'cause we're all supposed to love Jesus."

About that time, just before the plane was ready to leave, another man came and sat down on the aisle seat next to Cunningham and began to read a magazine. The little girl nudged Cunningham again and said, "Mister, ask him if he brushed his teeth this morning."

Cunningham was really uneasy with that one, and said that he didn't want to do it. But she kept nudging him and saying, "Ask him! Ask him!" So Cunningham turned to the man seated next to him and said, "Mister, I don't mean to bother you, but my friend here wants me to ask you if you brushed your teeth this morning."

The man looked startled, of course. But when he looked past Cunningham and saw the young girl sitting there, he could tell her good intentions. He took her question in stride and said with a smile, "Well, yes, I brushed my teeth this morning."

As the plane taxied onto the runway and began to take off, the young girl nudged Cunningham once more and said, "Ask him if he smokes." And so, good-naturedly, Cunningham did, and the man said that he didn't smoke.

As the plane was lifting into the air, the little girl nudged Cunningham once again and said, "Ask him if he loves Jesus."

Cunningham said, "I can't do that. That's too personal. I don't feel comfortable saying that to him."

But the girl smiled and insisted, "Ask him! Ask him!"

Cunningham turned to the fellow one more time and said, "Now she wants to know if you love Jesus."

The man could have responded like he had to the two previous questions—with a smile on his face and a little chuckle in his voice. And he almost did. But then the smile on his face disappeared, and his expression became serious. Finally he said to Cunningham, "You know, in all honesty, I can't say that I do. It's not that I don't want to, it's just that I don't know Him. I don't know how to know Him. I've wanted to be a person of faith all my life, but I haven't known how to do it. And now I've come to a time in my life when I really need that very much."

As the plane soared through the skies between Atlanta and Dallas, Milton Cunningham listened to the fellow talk about the brokenness in his life and shared his own personal story and testimony. He explained how to become a person of faith. He did that all because a little girl with Down syndrome had asked him to ask the fundamental question that all Christians should be finding a way to communicate: "Do you love Jesus?"

I was never so aware of the need to communicate my faith until I was a senior in college. One day the phone rang in my college dorm with the news that my Uncle J. C. had died an alcoholic's death on skid row in Chicago, and the family wanted me to do the funeral. I breathed a prayer that God would use me to be a witness to unsaved loved ones, packed my bags, loaded them and all the family into Dad's Buick, and headed for Chicago.

I hadn't been in the city forty-five minutes when God began to answer my prayers. Mom, Dad, Grandma Brewster, Terry, Richie, and I went downtown to the cemetery office to purchase a plot for Uncle J. C. Terry and I remained in the car with Richie, Uncle J. C.'s drinking pal. Richie looked at me and said, "You're a preacher, aren't you?"

"Yes," I replied, "I am a preacher. Why do you ask?"

He said, "I've been praying that God would send me a preacher. I don't want to be lost like J. C. I want to go to heaven. Can you help me, preacher?"

I told him yes, and then carefully and tenderly I began to share that receiving Jesus Christ is as simple as ABC:

A—**Admit that you have sinned.** And I read these words, "For all have sinned and fall short of the glory of God" (Rom. 3:23). Richie had no problem with that verse.

"I'm undesirable, unmentionable, and totally undone without God or His Son!" he said. "I'm a dirty rotten sinner!"

B—**Believe Him as Lord of your life.** "Yet to all who received him, to those who believed in his name, he gave the right to become children of God" (John 1:12).

C—**Confess Him as Lord of your life.** "That if you confess with your mouth, 'Jesus is Lord,' and believe in your heart that God raised him from the dead, you will be saved" (Rom. 10:9).

"Richie," I said, "are you willing to meet Christ on these terms?"

"I am," he said.

"Then let's pray." I began to lead him in prayer, and he repeated with me the following words:

> Dear Lord Jesus, I know I'm a sinner. I believe that You died for my sins and arose from the grave. I now turn

from my sins and invite You to come into my heart and
life. I receive You as my personal Savior, and I will follow
You as my Lord.

With the presence of God real and tears splashing down his cheeks
and onto the rubber floor mats in Daddy's Buick, Richie accepted
Christ. He was in a moment dramatically changed from undesirable
and undone to accepted and esteemed in the family of God!

About that time my mom, dad, and grandma came out and got
into the front seat of the car. I explained to them that Richie had been
saved, and if you have ever been to a camp meeting, you'll understand
what happened next. My grandmother started shouting, and the next
thing I knew my mother had joined in with praises to God.

As we returned to Grandma's house, everyone shared in the
excitement about Richie's acceptance of Christ. Then it happened.
Richie reached into his pocket and pulled out a Lucky Strike cigarette. The way I was raised, Christians didn't smoke. But no matter
who you were, *nobody* smoked in Daddy's Buick. I was stunned! He
had just been saved, and now he was smoking a cigarette.

After Richie had nearly finished smoking the first cigarette, he
turned to me and said, "I have a question for you, preacher. Now that
I have accepted Jesus, is it right or wrong for me to smoke cigarettes?"

Well, that question created a difficult situation, because I had to
think about the potential of discouraging my new convert.

"Richie," I said, "you know it could hurt your Christian witness." Unimpressed, he reached in and took out another cigarette
and lit it. Now, there were some doubters in Daddy's Buick! The
shouting had subsided.

"Preacher," he said, "I asked you a question. Is it right or wrong to smoke now that I have accepted Christ?"

Well, then I had a spark of inspiration because the Surgeon General had just come out with the warning on the back of the cigarette packs that cigarettes cause lung cancer. So I said to Richie, "Let me see your cigarette pack." I began to read from the back of his Lucky Strike pack that the Surgeon General had clearly stated that cigarettes could cause cancer. He was not impressed! For the third time, Richie took out a cigarette (obviously a chain smoker!).

He looked at me and said, "Preacher, I asked you a question. For the third time, is it right or wrong for me to smoke now that I have accepted Christ?"

Instantly, I began restating my position on smoking. "Richie," I replied, "first of all, it's not good for your witness; secondly, remember the Surgeon General said it is not good for your health." Suddenly, I had a moment of brilliance. "Richie," I said, "in my college class last week, my professor told us about Dr. Charles Hadden Spurgeon, the prince of preachers, the pastor of the great Metropolitan Tabernacle. Believe it or not, he was a smoker. But one day, he traveled downtown to the tobacco shop. To his surprise and amazement, the display case at the tobacco shop contained an advertisement with the type of tobacco Dr. Spurgeon smoked. When Spurgeon saw it on display, he said, 'I'll have no part of that. I'll quit smoking before I influence people in the wrong manner!'"

Richie was not moved. "Doesn't it say somewhere in the Bible that we are to cleanse ourselves from all filthiness of the flesh and spirit, perfecting holiness in the fear of God?"

"Yes, sir," I said, "it does!"

Richie said, "That's good enough for me. I quit!" With a sense of finality he crushed the last cigarette in the ashtray. Everyone in Daddy's Buick breathed a sigh of relief!

Several years after that, I was called to return to Chicago to conduct my aunt Shirley's funeral. I remember breathing the same prayer, "God, use me to be a witness to my unsaved loved ones." After arriving in Chicago, I went straight to the funeral home. My grandma Brewster hugged me and introduced me to Richie's mother. "How's Richie doing?" I asked her.

"Great," she replied. "He moved to Kentucky, got back with his wife and children. And, preacher, you'll never believe it. Richie not only has quit drinking, he hasn't smoked since your uncle J. C. passed away!"

Yes, here was a man who had been living on Chicago's skid row, selling his blood to buy cheap wine, someone who was undesirable and totally undone, praying that God would send him a preacher … and God sent him one at just the right moment. God is never late when you need grace!

God's grace is deep and powerful. A story I heard my mother share often in children's church when I was a child beautifully illustrates the incredible wonder of God's grace. A little boy's father had taught him how to carve toys out of driftwood. The boy's greatest accomplishment was making a boat, complete with sails, rigging, and rudder. The day came for him to test the water-worthiness of his boat. With great joy, he placed the boat in the water and watched it drift away as the breeze filled the sails. Suddenly, a strong gust of wind came up and broke the twine attached to the boat, and with no one around to help, he tearfully watched his prized boat sail out of reach and out of sight.

Days went by. One day as he approached a store where various toys were sold, he thought he saw his boat in the window. Realizing that it was *his* boat, he went in to identify it as his own creation. The shop owner told him that he would have to buy his boat back. Retreating, he counted his money and decided to purchase his boat. As the little guy walked out of the shop, the owner heard him say, "You are my boat twice over; I made you and now I have bought you."

Never forget that God made you and He wants to save you! Remember the words of this old hymn:

Amazing grace! How sweet the sound
that saved a wretch like me!
I once was lost, but now am found,
Was blind, but now I see.[19]

—John Newton

CHAPTER 7

Coping with Life When You Can't Even Figure Out Your Computer

Many people are doomed by what one might call a "Charlie Brown complex." Poor Charlie Brown can't do anything right. Of course, Lucy doesn't help. "You, Charlie Brown, are a foul ball in the line drive of life!" she often says.

Loud and clear!

Don't you wish you had some kind of warning when you're about to have a Charlie Brown day? I know I do. Maybe the following list will help you know what's coming around the corner.

You know it's going to be a bad day when:

1. You return from a vacation and discover a new name on your mailbox.
2. You stop at Motel 6 and they turn off the lights!
3. Your boss tells you not to bother taking off your coat.
4. You jump out of bed in the morning, and you miss the floor.

5. The bird singing outside your bedroom window is a buzzard.

6. Your dentures are locked together when you wake up in the morning.

7. Your horn accidentally gets stuck, and you're following a group of Hell's Angels on the freeway.

8. You put both contact lenses in the same eye.

9. You walk to work on a summer morning and find the bottom of your dress is tucked into the back of your panty hose.

10. You call your answering service, and they tell you it's none of your business.

11. Your income tax check bounces.

12. You put your bra or your athletic supporter on backwards and it fits better.

13. You step on your scale and it flashes, "Tilt, Tilt, Tilt."

14. The Suicide Prevention Hotline puts you on hold.

15. When the moving van starts to unload next door, the first four items down the ramp are dirt bikes.

16. Your pacemaker is recalled by the manufacturer.

17. Your church treasurer says, "The IRS called about some of your donations."

18. Your brakes go out just as a patrolman motions for you to pull over.

19. The university where you've willed your body
    to science calls to say they'd rather not
    wait.
20. You call the Suicide Prevention Hotline, and
    Dr. Kevorkian answers.

—Source Unknown

It was late Sunday evening, and what a full day it had been. I had preached twice, visited the hospital on an emergency call, and conducted a special board meeting concerning our building program. The moment I entered the church parsonage, the phone rang. I loosened my necktie, sat down at the hallway phone table, and answered with the weary voice of a tired pastor.

To my chagrin, it was Sister Bertha Runningmouth, and she had been talking to Brother Walkthehalls. She was just calling to register a complaint that many people in the church were upset with the new building program. For the next thirty minutes she took me to task on every facet of ministry. What a nightmare! Her voice was so shrill and so loud that I laid the phone down, and I could still hear her as she continued to hammer me.

Upstairs, my wife was giving our eighteen-month-old son, Seth, his evening bath. Bathing Seth was often a challenge; he loved to escape from the bathtub when his mother was not looking, and this night was no exception. As Sister Bertha droned on, I heard Linda's saintly voice yelling, "Seth Aaron Toler, come back here!" (All mothers mean business when they use the child's middle name!)

Startled, I looked up and discovered Seth sliding down the stairs headfirst, naked, and yelling for me at the top of his voice. He stood up quickly and headed for me. Undaunted by the noise in the background, Sister Bertha kept on talking. By this time, Seth was climbing into my lap, soaking wet. He shivered and shook his curly blond head, and water covered my blue Sunday suit. But he wasn't finished. He gave me a somewhat toothless grin, hugged me, and kissed me on each cheek. "Daddy," he said, "I wuv you!" His mother, not far behind, caught up! She wrapped him in a bath towel and off they went to complete his bath, oblivious to the fact that I had been in great need of a hug!

Tears streamed down my cheeks, and the frown that creased my face turned to a smile as Sister Bertha finalized her Sunday evening fireside chat with me. In that moment, only one thing mattered. I knew I was loved. God was not late when I needed encouragement!

Perhaps you have heard the story of the fellow who was about to jump from a bridge. An alert police officer slowly and methodically moved toward him, talking with him all the time. When he got within inches of the man, he said, "Surely nothing could be bad enough for you to take your life. Tell me about it. Talk to me."

The would-be jumper told how his wife had left him, how his business had become bankrupt, how his friends had deserted him. Everything in life had lost meaning. For thirty minutes he told the sad story. Then they both jumped!

I love *The Far Side* cartoon series. A recent cartoon pictured two cowboys out on the range and illustrates how contagious discouragement can be. One cowboy says to the other, "The buffalo is the ugliest animal in the world." Nearby a buffalo is heard to say, "I think I've just heard a discouraging word!"

At times we all suffer with bouts of discouragement. Are you suffering from discouragement right now? It may be from a relationship that's gone sour, a job that's been lost, or the death of a loved one. Without doubt, negative people and negative circumstances can combine to stifle our spiritual lives.

Writer Alexandra Kropotkin once described the death of her friend: "One day a millionaire of my acquaintance, whose pride it was never to offer a tip for any service, faced an unforgettable tragedy. His chief accountant committed suicide. The books were found to be in perfect order; the affairs of the dead man, a modest bachelor, were prosperous and calm. The only letter left by the accountant was a brief note to his millionaire employer. It read: 'In thirty years I have never had one word of encouragement. I'm fed up.'"[20]

Discouragement comes when you try to start with what you wish
you had but don't have. And it intensifies when you insist on trying
to be in a position you are not in and probably never will be in.[21]
—Stuart Briscoe

During the Boer War (1889–1902), a man was convicted of a very unusual crime: being a "discourager." The South African town of Ladysmith had been under attack, and this traitor had moved up and down the lines of soldiers who were defending the city doing everything he could to discourage them. He pointed out the enemy's strength, the difficulty of defending against them, and the inevitable capture of the city. He hadn't used a gun in his attack. It hadn't been necessary. His weapon had been the power of discouragement.

Encouragement, on the other hand, can be a powerful friend. It strengthens the weak, imparts courage to the fainthearted, and gives hope to the faltering. If you want a ministry in the church where there's little or no competition, then become an encourager. Almost everyone wants to be the soloist in the choir. Or the lead in the Easter play. Or the director of the men's or ladies' ministries. But there aren't a whole lot of applicants signing up for the Ministry of Encouragement. You want job security in church work? Become a Barnabas.

The apostle Paul gave us four ways to handle any discouragement we might experience in life. The following Scripture verse offers a foolproof formula for overcoming discouragement: "Therefore, since through God's mercy we have this ministry, we do not lose heart" (2 Cor. 4:1).

THE MERCY OF GOD

In 1984, I was privileged to travel around the world for World Relief Corporation and World Gospel Mission, visiting refugee camps and speaking to and encouraging mission leaders on matters of leadership, church growth, and evangelism. I also visited many of the great growing churches of the world. Upon arrival in Seoul, South Korea, Linda and I and our dear friends David and Mary Vaughn caught a taxi and headed to the Full Gospel Central Church. A mutual friend, Dr. Holland London Sr., had made special arrangements for us to visit Dr. David (Paul) Cho's office and church. Dr. Cho's administrative assistant, Miss Lee, gave us a tour of the huge twenty-five-thousand-seat sanctuary and the additional education units on the church property.

It was especially exhilarating to observe two thousand people in line on Tuesday morning waiting to be baptized! Miss Lee informed us that this was an everyday occurrence and a direct answer to the prayers of God's people. We were greatly moved by the phenomenal growth of the great church under the leadership of Dr. Cho. Later, we attended the Sunday services. Dr. Cho told of how the church began with a small tent and five people. As he continued to reflect on the history of this great church, he said, "I became so discouraged in 1969 when we were building the new sanctuary that I went to the eighteenth floor of the educational building and contemplated jumping out!"

Unbelievable! This man who pastors the largest church in the world (last count was eight hundred thousand members) became so discouraged that he felt like ending his life! But God was faithful. Dr. Cho said, "God came to my rescue; just in the midst of my discouragement He brought peace and encouragement!"

THE COMFORT OF GOD AND FRIENDS

The apostle Paul, who had been stoned, shipwrecked, beaten, bitten by a snake, and spat upon, had the first answer to discouragement: "Though outwardly we are wasting away, yet inwardly we are being renewed day by day. For our light and momentary troubles are achieving for us an eternal glory that far out weighs them all" (2 Cor. 4:16–17). "But God, who comforts the downcast, comforted us by the coming of Titus" (2 Cor. 7:6). Apparently, Paul was somewhat frightened about the future. He realized that life was passing by quickly, but he found comfort from God and Titus. God always has someone to speak words of comfort when you are literally scared to death. God has never failed to bring comfort during my darkest hours.

There was a time early in my ministry when I was going to quit! I was so discouraged that I began reading the classified ads in the newspaper, looking for a new career. In the midst of my discouragement, my mother came to town to spend the weekend. On Friday evening with tear-filled eyes, I told Mother that I was going to leave the ministry. Instantly, she got out of her La-Z-Boy rocker, walked over to me, placed her hands on my head, and began to pray, "God, You called my son into the ministry, You anointed him to preach the gospel. Devil, you take your hands off my son, in Jesus' name, and God, encourage Stanley right now." Let me tell you, a new determination and energy flowed immediately through my inner being. God brought comfort through my dear mother—the only person to ever call me Stanley.

Pastor and theologian Richard Niebuhr was teaching a class. Near the end of the lecture he said, "Whatever comes into our lives, God can turn around for good." In that same class was a student who, just a few weeks before, had been involved in a boating accident. The student had lost his mother and father, his only sibling, and his fiancée. He alone had survived. There were those in the class who thought Dr. Niebuhr was either crazy or simply insensitive to the events of the past weeks.

The lecture ended, and all the students stayed, expecting to see the grieving young man angrily accuse the professor of making such an insensitive theological statement. But what happened surprised them all. The student walked up to Dr. Niebuhr, shook his hand, and said, "Thank you, sir. That is the only thing that makes life worthwhile." He then turned and walked away.

It is true. God is good. But that does not mean that bad things will not happen. Floods come, the earth quakes, people die, and marriages break up. We cry, but so does God. Remember the powerful words of Isaiah 53:4 as Isaiah foretold the coming of the Messiah: "Surely he took up our infirmities and carried our sorrows." When we hurt, God cares. When we are in pain, God is present to comfort. When alone, God can be a strengthening companion.

If you need comfort this very moment, consider the words of the old hymn "God Will Take Care of You":

(Verse 1)
Be not dismayed whate'er betide,
God will take care of you;
beneath His wings of love abide,
God will take care of you.

(Verse 4)
No matter what will be the test,
God will take care of you;
Lean, weary one, upon His breast,
God will take care of you.
Thro' ev'ry day, o'er all the way;
He will take care of you,
God will take care of you.[22]

Dietrich Bonhoeffer in his book *The Cost of Discipleship* noted, "Christians have forgotten the ministry of listening that has been committed to them by the One who is Himself the great listener." This great scholar challenged every believer to improve his or her listening skills.

After reading Bonhoeffer's book, I began to implement the following methods as a part of my encouragement ministry:

Writing letters. Several years ago, I read an article in *Guideposts* magazine titled "The Power of a Note," written by Norman Vincent Peale. It challenged Christians to write "short, spontaneous, specific notes of encouragement." Since reading Peale's article, I have practiced this ritual of comfort, and I might add that I have the worst handwriting in the world! Recently, I wrote a note of encouragement to a friend who claims he took it to the local pharmacist to be deciphered. They gave him a prescription for Valium! So, even if he couldn't read my note, he got a great laugh at my expense!

Talk-show host Larry King reported that during his hospital stay he had many letters and gifts. King mentioned on his TV show that the letter that touched him the most was the one sent by Pete Maravich, former NBA star. Peter included a Bible and the following note: "Dear Larry, I'm so glad to hear that everything went well with your surgery. I want you to know that God was watching over you every minute, and even though I know you may question that, I also know that one day it will be revealed to you ... because He lives."

One week later, King noted, Pete Maravich, college basketball and NBA luminary, died.

Pastor Greg Asimakoupoulos states, "I keep a handy file folder of short notes and cards from individuals in my desk drawer. These notes provide a quick resource of encouragement when doubt or congregational turmoil bring discouragement." After hearing this, I began the same practice. What a lift it can bring on a dark, cloudy day!

Compassionate listening. In a book titled *The Power of Encouragement,* author Jean Doering tells the story a little girl who went to comfort the mother of a playmate who had recently died. When she returned home, her mother asked what she had done to comfort the mother of her playmate. She said, "I just climbed up in her lap and cried with her." Ask God to give you a compassionate heart!

The touch of the hand. The day had finally arrived. Eighty-two-year-old Dr. Paul S. Rees, great expositor and ministry statesman, was speaking at the annual ministerial convention. Dr. Rees was a model preacher for me. I had listened to his tapes, read his books, and was finally getting the chance to meet him! I was more than a little excited. We had named our newborn son, Seth, after Dr. Rees's father, Seth Cook Rees.

The break time was my chance to greet Dr. Rees. After waiting in line for fifteen minutes, my turn came. I shook hands with him and told him about our new son, Seth. Dr. Rees asked, "Do you have a picture of your son?" As any proud father would, I instantly produced a photo of my son. "What a good-looking little guy!" Dr. Rees said. "Would it be okay if I pray for him?"

"Of course," I replied. "Please do so!" Dr. Rees proceeded to place his hand over the picture of Seth in my outstretched hand and prayed a brief but sensitive prayer. I cried like a baby, and so did other ministers waiting in the same line.

When I returned home, I shared with Linda what had taken place. We wept together in appreciation for the prayer of blessing by Dr. Rees. After experiencing the prayerful touch from the hand of Dr. Paul S. Rees, I decided that I would take parishioners by the hand

and pray with them as they shared with me their joys and sorrows. There is power in the touch for us. Martin Luther once said, "We are all little Christs—when we touch, He touches."

Several years ago on the campus of Southern Nazarene University, where I formerly served as pastor-in-residence, we held a conference for ministers. One of the speakers, Dr. Morris Weigelt, shared about a time of deep depression in his life. I was especially touched when he talked about a night during his hospitalization. Morris told the group of ministers that during the middle of the night "all of his insecurities and depression came upon him."

Weigelt got out of bed and walked the halls looking for someone awake and willing to give him a hug. With a great deal of pathos and humor, he concluded that all he could find was a huge, burly security guard. "Sir," he said, "would you give me a hug?"

"I sure will!" the security guard responded. Dr. Weigelt indicated that he found comfort and encouragement from the touch of the big, burly security guard. He returned to his room and slept peacefully.

Lord, make me an instrument of Thy peace;
Where there is hatred, let me sow love;
Where there is injury, pardon;
Where there is discord, harmony
Where there is doubt, faith;
Where there is despair, hope;
Where there is darkness, light;
Where there is sadness, joy.
O Divine Master, grant that I may
not so much seek to be consoled as to console;

to be loved as to love;

for it is in giving that we receive,

it is in pardoning, that we are pardoned,

it is in dying, that we are born to Eternal Life.

Amen.

—The Peace Prayer of St. Francis

CONFIDENCE IN OUR FUTURE WITH CHRIST

Paul said in 2 Corinthians 5:5, "Now it is God who has made us for his very purpose and has given us the Spirit as a deposit, guaranteeing what is to come."

My friend Talmadge Johnson told the story of the man who stopped to watch a Little League baseball game. He asked one of the youngsters what the score was. "We're losing 18-0," was the answer.

"Well," said the man, "I must say you don't look discouraged."

"Discouraged?" the boy said, puzzled. "Why should we be discouraged? We haven't come to bat yet."

THE COURAGE TO TAKE A GIANT STEP OF FAITH

You have the power of choice! You can choose to be discouraged, depressed, and live life in a dark, dingy dungeon. Or you can go out on a limb with God and make a commitment to move forward with God.

In his lectures, Carl Sandburg often included the story of seven-year-old Abe Lincoln. One evening, Abe walked over to his cabin door and opened it. He looked up into the face of the full moon and said, "Mr. Moon, what do you see from way up there?"

Mr. Moon answered, "Abe, I see a calendar and it says 1816. I see eight million people in the United States of America. I see sixteen thousand covered wagons plodding slowly across the Midwestern plains toward California. And, Abe, I see far to the west a wagon in the desert between two ridges of the Rocky Mountains. The wagon is broken, weeds are crawling in the spokes, and there is an old dusty skeleton nearby with a pair of empty moccasins and some dry bones. I also see a sign that says 'The cowards never started!'"

Why not rely on the promises of God and choose to be encouraged rather than discouraged?

Dell once released a computer it dubbed "easy to use." Admittedly, I'm skeptical of the claim. I've never been able to figure out my computer! It works beautifully. It's too bad I've never actually been able to get it to work the way I wanted. I may not be able to figure out my computer, but one thing I am sure about: If God says it in His Word, that settles it for me! My encouragement is not in the guarantees and empty promises of this world! It is in my future with Christ!

> *How great is the love the Father has lavished on us, that we should be called children of God! And that is what we are! The reason the world does not know us is that it did not know him. Dear friends, now we are children of God, and what we will be has not yet been made known. But we know that when he appears, we shall be like him, for we shall see him as he is. Everyone who has this hope in him purifies himself, just as he is pure. (1 John 3:1–3)*

CHAPTER 8

Humor Keeps Getting in the Way of My Depression

Are you like the guy who said a while back, "I've got so many troubles that if anything bad happens to me today, it'll be two weeks before I can worry about it"? Or is your situation more like that of a fellow who once received some "encouragement" from Hagar the Horrible in the popular cartoon strip. In the first frame, it looks like this fellow is so far down that he needs a periscope to see what shoes he's wearing, and Hagar is trying to cheer him up. So Hagar says, "Today the world dumped on you." Next he says, "Today the world humiliated you." In the third frame, his poor friend is sobbing uncontrollably, and Hagar says philosophically, "Well, tomorrow is another day."

WE'RE ALL IN THE SAME VIKING SHIP

Hagar's friend is not alone. All of us have felt dumped on, humiliated, or abused in life at one time or another. (If you think you haven't, then you'd better put a quarter in one of those blood pressure machines in your local drug store to see if you still have a pulse!)

Use the following checklist to measure your depression quotient. You know you are depressed when …

- The cloud that's been following you around has been picked up by Doppler radar and is featured on the six o'clock weather report.
- You start crying uncontrollably during the Bonus Round of *Jeopardy*.
- You've just driven sixty-eight miles in the fast lane of the freeway with your left-turn signal flashing.
- It's three a.m., and you're watching the "Melon Baller Hour" on QVC.
- The most exciting part of your day is counting the ceiling tiles in your bedroom.
- You've got a five o'clock shadow, and you don't care—and you're a woman.
- You've ordered every product featured on every infomercial on television. Twice.
- While talking to yourself, you realize you're not even interested in what you have to say.

Many events can trigger a bout of depression. Even if you're not feeling depressed today, you may feel downhearted if one of the following things happen to you:

- Your credit card gets rejected at the church car wash.
- You win the Publisher's Clearing House Sweepstakes, but you mistake the Prize Patrol for Jehovah's Witnesses and don't open the door.
- Your employer, who three months ago said you were indispensable, suddenly dispenses of you.
- Your daughter elopes with the leader of a motorcycle gang who has twice as many tattoos as brain cells.
- You're the lead car in a one-hundred-car pileup.
- You discover your date has a mate in another state.

- Your accountant calls from his new condo in Acapulco to tell you you're broke.
- The electric company shuts off your power in the middle of a dinner party for your new in-laws.
- You're at the end of your rope ... and you suddenly realize it's a live electric cord and you're standing in water.

For most of us, it comes as little surprise to learn that according to the American Psychological Association, over 18 million people in this country are under a doctor's care—receiving either cognitive or chemical therapy, or both—for depression. (It's even been rumored that in the story of Snow White, there were really only six dwarfs. Happy was just Grumpy on Prozac.)

Despite what you may think, depression isn't just a phenomenon of present day. Despair, discouragement, and depression have been around since ancient days. The condition cuts a wide swath and can range from occasional bouts of mild sadness or self-pity about the way things have been going lately to complete mental, psychological, and spiritual exhaustion leading to severe malaise or even attempts of suicide.

Have you ever found yourself at home in the middle of the day staring at the walls and crying for no reason? Do you go to the mailbox each morning, fearing what bad news or unexpected bill lie inside it? Do you count the seconds on the clock until you can leave your job, classes, or other responsibilities just so you can go straight home to close the curtains and recover? Do you suffer chronic aches and pains that have no physical origin or cause? Or maybe you're experiencing an emotional state that brings on a debilitating, defeating, deepening gloom that immobilizes you until life seems to both stand still and race by at once. If so, you might very well be depressed, and you ought to begin talking to a friend, a loved one, or a trained counselor about this potential spiral.

Years ago, the late Joe Bayly wrote something he called "Psalm in a Hotel Room." It may capture your current state of mind if you're feeling down and out:

I'm alone, Lord,
alone
a thousand miles from home.
There's no one here who knows my name
except the clerk
and he spelled it wrong;
no one to eat dinner with,
laugh at my jokes,
listen to my gripes,
be happy with me about what happened today,
and say that's great.
No one cares.
There's just this lousy bed
and slush in the street outside
between the buildings.
I feel sorry for myself
and I've plenty of reason to.
Maybe I ought to say
"I'm on top of it,
praise the Lord,

things are great,"
but they're not.
Tonight,
it's all gray slush.

You Are Not Alone

For too long, people in the Christian world have believed and taught the myth that depression is a sin for Christians. If that's true, then most of the people in the Bible were terrible sinners. Jeremiah had his bout with depression. In the twentieth chapter of Jeremiah, he said,

> *Oh LORD, you deceived me, and I was deceived; you overpowered me and prevailed. I am ridiculed all day long; everyone mocks me. Whenever I speak, I cry out proclaiming violence and destruction. So the word of the LORD has brought me insult and reproach all day long. But if I say, "I will not mention him or speak any more in his name," his word is in my heart like a fire, a fire shut up in my bones. I am weary of holding it in; indeed, I cannot. I hear many whisperings, "Terror on every side! Report him! Let's report him!" All my friends are waiting for me to slip, saying, "Perhaps he will be deceived; then we will prevail over him and take our revenge on him." (Jer. 20:7–10)*

I believe that is the voice of a tremendous man of God—experiencing tremendous depression.

Job certainly felt like he was on the short end of the uplift stick. Hallmark doesn't even make a card for all the troubles he had to face. And what about Jonah? I doubt if he was singing "Whistle a Happy Tune" from the belly of that whale.

David wrote in his songs, "Why are you downcast, O my soul? Why so disturbed within me?" (Ps. 42:5); "O LORD, how many are my foes! How many rise up against me! Many are saying of me, 'God will not deliver him'" (Ps. 3:1–2); "O LORD, do not rebuke me in your anger or discipline me in your wrath. Be merciful to me, LORD, for I am faint; O LORD, heal me, for my bones are in agony. My soul is in anguish. How long, O LORD, how long?" (Ps. 6:1–3).

Even after an incredible victory that he had fought hard to win at Mount Carmel, Elijah found himself too depressed to celebrate. Apparently alone in the gore that follows brutal war, standing among fallen soldiers on both sides, Elijah put his head between his knees and cried (1 Kings 18:42).

It was no different during New Testament times. The apostle Peter felt he had destroyed the life of Christ in his betrayal. Paul went to Corinth in "weakness and fear, and with much trembling" (1 Cor. 2:3). And after his remarkable successes in the building of God's kingdom, he felt down. Having proclaimed the good news of the gospel to much of Asia, Paul wrote to the church at Corinth, "We do not want you to be uninformed, brothers, about the hardships we suffered in the province of Asia. We were under great pressure, far beyond our ability to endure, so that we despaired even of life" (2 Cor. 1:8). Even Christ cried out in the garden, "My soul is overwhelmed with sorrow to the point of death" (Matt. 26:38).

Don't Compound Depression with Unnecessary Guilt

David A. Seamands wrote in his book *Healing for Damaged Emotions* that by "denying their depression, many Christians add to their troubles. They add guilt on top of the depression and thereby double the problem." He went on to conclude, "Depression is not necessarily a sign of spiritual failure."[23]

Depression seems to be nature's emotional backlash, a reaction like the wallop from firing a gun of heavy caliber. As Seamands said, "It's nature's recoil, or perhaps the balance wheel in what C. S. Lewis calls 'the law of undulation' in the human personality."[24] Depression is related to personality structure, physical makeup, body chemistry, glandular functions, emotional patterns, and learned feeling concepts.

Seamands went on to say that "sin may lead to depression, but all depression does not come from sin."[25] How can you tell the difference between something that comes from sin and something that doesn't? He said that concrete, specific feelings of guilt that can be related to a particular, precise act or attitude are often reliably traced back to something that is wrong. The emotions that follow can be real guilt and real depression resulting from a real transgression.

On the other hand, a vague, all-inclusive umbrella of self-accusation and general feelings of anxiety and condemnation that cannot be pinpointed are often signs of pseudoguilt or just plain depression that has come from other emotional sources. Therefore, he concluded that the most important and "first step in learning to live above depression is to accept yourself as you are. This is not to say that you are to be controlled by your temperament.... You cannot."[26]

ONE THING JORDAN COULDN'T SLAM DUNK

Depression is a timeless, universal plague. It is not a yuppie disease brought on by busy schedules and overpriced lifestyles. It affects people from Brooklyn to Brazil, Greenland to Greenpeace, homeless to high society. Basketball legend Michael Jordan has even experienced depression. Here's what he had to say about it:

> I went to my room and I closed the door and I cried. For a while, I couldn't stop. Even though there was no one else home at the time, I kept the door shut. It was important to me that no one hear me or see me.

> For about two weeks, every boy who had tried out for the basketball team knew what day the cut list was going to go up. We knew that it was going to be posted in the gym, in the morning.

> So that morning we all went in there, and the list was up. I had a friend—his name was Leroy Smith—and we went in to look at the list together. We stood there and looked for our names.

> Leroy's name was on the list. He made it. Mine wasn't on the list.[27]

No doubt at that moment Michael Jordan contemplated giving up basketball. Lucky for the NBA, he didn't allow depression or discouragement to overpower his dreams.

DEPRESSION IS NO RESPECTER OF POSITION OR CLASS

During World War II, Winston Churchill, the great leader of Britain, frequently addressed the people of England, encouraging them never to give up. Yet they say that time and time again, when he turned off the microphone, he sank into a deep, dark depression.

Charles Spurgeon, one of the great orators and preachers of the faith, had a life filled with depression. He once said, "Before any great achievement, some major depression [would come] upon me." This comment came from the man who pastored one of the largest churches in all of Christendom: "I took to the lowliest steps. I uttered my misery to God and I found no room for glory on excelsius."

In his book *Living Beyond the Daily Grind,* noted author and speaker Dr. Charles Swindoll wrote about a day he'll never forget:

> Many years ago when I was living in Dallas, I received a phone call which led me to a tiny and dirty garage apartment. I was met at the screen door by a man with a 12-gauge shotgun. He invited me in. We sat for over an hour at a tiny kitchen table with a naked light bulb hanging above it. He poured out a heart-breaking story.
>
> He had just been released from the hospital, recovering from back surgery. He was alone, having lost contact with his wife and their only son. As we talked of the man's intense struggles, I noticed that his small apartment was full of pictures—all of them of his son at various stages of growth.

There were photos taken of the boy when he was still in diapers. Others were with his dad when the lad was graduating from kindergarten. Still others showed him in his Little League uniform with a bat over his shoulder … on and on, right up through high school. The man's entire focus centered upon a marriage that had failed and especially a boy he no longer was able to enjoy. Those nostalgic "misty, water-colored memories of the way we were" held him captive in a prisonhouse of despondency.

Unfortunately, my attempts to help him see beyond the walls of his anguish proved futile. In less than a week, he shot himself to death in his car which he had driven deep into the woods in East Texas.[28]

Depression is particularly difficult for the elderly, whose physical faculties are declining at a pace that can be frightening. I can identify with this group. Our memories are fading. We're constantly getting our ATM secret code mixed up with our blood pressure count, and the only bench pressing we do now is in the park when we sit on one. Our reflexes are slower, too. We've been seen at ball games jumping up to catch a fly ball that was hit in the previous inning!

Depression can appear in many different ways for the aging. Sometimes it's evidenced by a critical or negative attitude. Other times it's a feeling—unfounded, of course—of being unwanted and in the way.

ONE APPROACH TO OVERCOMING DEPRESSION

Reader's Digest published an article a few years ago titled "How to Beat a Bad Mood" that offers many tried-and-true methods for overcoming a sense of "low tide."

The first secret mentioned in the article is exercise. As mentioned previously, regular exercise is one of the few free, nonprescription antidepressants to which we have access. The physical response to muscle use and exertion enables the body to get a "natural high," a feeling of well-being and satisfaction.

However, there are those who can turn even healthy exercise into something that causes depression instead of curing it. For some reason, in our culture we have begun to take some things a bit too seriously. In the last couple of decades, the fitness industry has fed one of America's top obsessions—and as with almost all obsessions, there is the probability of letdown and depression. For instance, bicycling used to be a traditional childhood enjoyment—you'd hop on your bike, ride over to Tooly's house, play catch for a few minutes, ride to the local playground for a couple of hours of baseball, then ride home mad because Tooly called you out at home plate.

Today, bicycling is a multimillion-dollar industry. Adults have messed it up with their competition to have the best, be the fastest, get written up in *Psycho-Cycle Magazine,* and die pedaling. There are now bicycles made of less metal than my son's braces, but which cost twice as much. There are cycling helmets, cycling gloves, cycling shirts, cycling shoes, cycling water bags, cycling mirrors, cycling watches, odometers, and worst of the worst, cycling shorts (although it is nice that they finally found a use for all those old tourniquets).

What's funny about this cycling craze—or tragic, depending on your outlook—is the scowl that "career riders" give the rest of us when we pass them by in our plaid Wal-Mart cutoffs and worn-out baseball cap turned backward—as if *we* were giving bike riding a bad name.

Then, there are the bicycle rallies, races, and weekend retreats held all over the country. As a result of all of this, it is only natural for folks to set extremely high goals, unreachable goals in many cases, and when those sights go unmet, depression sets in.

Sometimes I suspect that the exercise and fashion industries are working together to make people feel inadequate. The standard of fitness in magazines and television translates into extreme thinness and malnourishment. It seems only fitting that as a result of the media's obsession with "the perfect body," the incidence of eating disorders—forms of depression, themselves—has increased astronomically.

Statistics show that 90 percent of all cases of bulimia and anorexia nervosa occur among women. Women have been specifically targeted by advertisers with their message "To get thin is to fit in," and as a result, women have taken the message of television and magazines to such a level that many of them die of starvation.

While we're at it, let's talk about another characteristic of the perfect Hollywood physique: a dark tan. Historically, the shade of a person's tan indicated social status. Tanned skin was associated with working-class income—planting, harvesting, building, etc. Conversely, pale skin untouched by the sun was a sign of affluence, an indication that a person was wealthy enough not to have to work at all.

Today, however, things have reversed. Because most Americans work indoors under artificial fluorescent lighting, a tanned body is associated with a life of leisure and relaxation at the beach or on a boat—in other words, a life of wealth. Again, advertisers have capitalized on this by portraying healthy and popular people as tanned (and thin and riding a bicycle) so that anyone not sporting a forty-third grade of brownness is out of the proverbial loop—and the alienation caused by such feelings is a typical cause of depression. And of course, tanning salons have shot up all across the country in an effort to make money on this fad, and lotions and tanning oils are giving vitamin sales a run for their money.

But back to *Reader's Digest's* suggestions on how to make your mood more positive. One of the article's suggestions is to avoid wearing red clothes. We're not sure why red is a downer, because most of us enjoy seeing red clothes, especially on our sweethearts and firemen, but for some folks, apparently, red is associated with the target of a charging bull or the monthly statement of an over-charging spouse.

The third suggestion of the article is to listen to good music. It's that word, "good," that throws most of us. Now to our teenage sons, good music is not really music at all. It's more like loud noises recorded during a New York City traffic jam while a nearby building is being imploded. To a teenage boy, it's not music unless it starts to cause the paint to flake off the walls!

ON THE LIGHTER SIDE ...

Now all three of the above suggestions are good, but I still believe the best way to beat a bad mood is to just *lighten up*. Sound overly simplistic? Well, it's the truth. Your failures will not stop the earth from spinning any more than your successes will keep it going.

Barbara Johnson, author of *Mama, Get the Hammer! There's a Fly on Papa's Head!* says there are some things you should never do when you're feeling blue. First, never weigh yourself. To that, we'd add, never look in the mirror after a Sunday church dinner—unless you want to see how closely related "potluck" and "potbelly" really are.

Barbara also suggests not watching *Old Yeller* when you're down. To that I'd have to say ditto with *Titanic*. Let's face it, the boat sank. Hundreds of people died. Celine Dion's heart may go on, but yours is just going to break. And if you're already feeling down, it'd be better to watch a comedy instead. I'd recommend *The Three Stooges, I Love Lucy*, or live coverage of Congress in session.

Barbara recommends avoiding reading your high school or college yearbooks, any poem by Emily Dickinson, or the entire book of Lamentations. She advises not going near a chocolate shop, opening your credit card bills (or any envelope with a window in it, for that matter), or going shopping for a swimsuit when you're down. That's good advice. For most of us, swimsuits are like false friends. As soon as your back is turned, they'll expose all your faults.

TALK ABOUT IT

One of the first steps to recovering from depression is telling God how you feel. That may not be the way you were raised, the way you were taught to pray, but it is a right response to despondency. Be open. If you want to ask God why your loved one had to die, why your children aren't choosing the right paths, or why life is so tough at times, go ahead and ask Him. God understands your heart, your anger, your doubts. He knows. He's been there too.

You should also open up to your friends and express the feelings that have pressed you down. Even those who believe that sanctification prevents us from showing anger must acknowledge that when we are depressed, it's healthier to just let it out. Jesus, on the cross in front of His followers, let His feelings surface. If our Lord practiced this kind of openness, shouldn't we? Don't forget how He cleared the temple, turning over tables and cracking a whip!

Many of us never knew we were allowed to speak our feelings, to take off our masks of perfection and be real, imperfectly real. If only we would do this, though. If we could talk openly to a trusted friend or minister, we'd feel a lot better. But beware of those who use the guise of accountability to gather tidbits of gossip. They may take your need to the Lord, but on the way they'll pass it along to half the church.

And no matter what, never give up. Many people crumble under stress and pressure because they think they have to carry their troubles alone. They forget that God is already carrying most of the load. All they have to do is let go. In chapter 20 of Jeremiah, the prophet realized, "The LORD is with me like a mighty warrior; so my persecutors will stumble and not prevail" (v. 11). David concluded in Psalm 23, "The LORD is my shepherd, I shall not be in want" (v. 1). Paul stated in Philippians 4:11–13, "I have learned to be content whatever the circumstances. I know what it is to be in need, and I know what it is to have plenty. I have learned the secret of being content in any and every situation, whether well fed or hungry, whether living in plenty or in want. I can do all things through him who gives me strength."

PASS IT ON

Perhaps you are not fighting depression, but you know someone who is—possibly a young person you feel called to help. Well-known writer and speaker Josh McDowell provided some advice that will help you. He has identified six steps to support a down person. And to make them memorable, he used them to form the acronym LEADER.

Listen. Either through prayer, patient encouragement, sincere questions, or frequent reassurances, we need to let depressed people vent their frustrations to someone.

Empathize. The adage "Walk a mile in his shoes" is never truer than it is when dealing with depressed people. The secret, though, is not to develop a sense of dependence with a depressed person but independence.

Affirm. Unconditional affirmation and acceptance of the person is imperative for recovery.

Direct. Give sound advice and instruction. Sing, be thankful, and help others lean on God. Help them rest in the Spirit.

Enlist. The person who feels down has to buy into the recovery process. It is imperative to use his or her own resolve, initiative, imagination, and participation to make it happen.

Refer. Provide a sense of long-term security by referring the individual to a psychologist, psychiatrist, or support group.[29]

With all due respect to Josh McDowell, I'd like to add a seventh step: *hug.* (It doesn't work with the acronym, but it's too important to leave out.) Not long ago, a Sunday school teacher asked her class of adult students, "Does anyone need a hug today?" Toward the middle of the room, a single parent meekly raised her hand, so the teacher walked across the room and picked up a large teddy bear that had been sitting in a child's rocker and carried it to the woman.

"Would you hold this bear?" the teacher asked.

Immediately, the woman clasped the bear tightly to her and held onto it for a long time—throughout the entire lesson, as a matter of fact.

Hugs are to depression, spiritual pain, and emotional distress what aspirin is to a toothache, what antacid is to a stomachache, and what an eraser is to my golf scorecard! Hugs are soothing, reassuring, and tangible reminders that you have value.

There's a lovely little song that you may have learned when you were younger—it puts the meaning of a hug into a memorable rhyme:

> *It's wondrous what a hug can do.*
> *A hug can cheer you when you're blue.*
> *A hug can say, "I love you so."*

Or "Gee! I hate to see you go."
A hug is, "Welcome back again!" and
"Great to see you" or "Where've you been?"
The hug! There's just no doubt about it,
We surely couldn't survive without it.

—Dean Walley

Though I can't do it in person, I'd like to extend a hug to you right now. God loves you, and so do I. Now pass that hug along today to someone else who can use it.

CHAPTER 9

All May Be Fair in Love and War,
but Not Much in Life Is!

My longtime friend Chuck Crow loves to tell the story of the old man who was dying while his wife of more than fifty years watched at his bedside. Fred opened his eyes and saw Martha. "There you are, Martha," he said, "at my side once again."

"Yes, dear," Martha said.

"In retrospect," the old man said, "I remember all the times that you've been at my side. You were there when I was drafted and had to go off to fight in the Korean War. You were there with me when our first house burned to the ground. And you were there when I had the accident that destroyed our little Volkswagen. Yes, you were there when our little shoe shop went belly-up and I lost every cent I had."

"Yes, honey," his wife said, patting his hand.

Fred sighed deeply. "You know, Martha," he said, "you're bad luck!"

Marriage is a strange and wonderful thing. It is difficult to find a more basic problem than our confusion about human relations. Not long ago I attended a marriage seminar taught by widely known counselor Norman Wright. Dr. Wright pointed out two basic reasons that relationships fail: *fear*, which causes us to erect barriers; and *selfishness*, which causes us to focus on fulfilling our own needs instead of the needs of others.

Dr. Wright also discussed three vital qualities that enable us to develop lasting relationships: *genuineness*, which enables us to be who we are without a facade; *nonpossessive love*, which enables us to accept a person as he or she is and allow him or her space; and *empathy*, which enables us to feel with another person.[30]

Relationships are funny things. And perhaps nothing captures their peculiarities with greater humor than country music. As Paul Schmed said in an article titled "Ever Had an Achy Breaky Heart?" the smash hit by Billy Ray Cyrus was just one of the many country-music songs to put into words the woeful feelings of a love gone bad. But country music has been doing that for decades. Check out some of these countrified, lost-love lines passed down through the years:

"Flushed from the bathroom of your heart"
—Jack Clement, 1967

"I only miss you on days that end in 'Y"
—Jim Malloy, 1975

"How come your dog don't bite nobody but me?"
—Wayne Walker and Mel Tillis, 1961

"My tears have washed 'I love you' from the blackboard of my heart."
—Hank Thompson and Lyle Gaston, 1956.

Of course, country music isn't all bad news. Some of the love songs that come from the hills are quite—well—uplifting. Wouldn't you just love to hear your date say:

> *"Old King Kong was just a little monkey*
> *compared to my love for you"*
> —Sammy Lyons, 1977

> *"If I don't love you, grits ain't groceries"*
> —George Jones, 1959

Had enough? If not, check out the book *I've Got Tears in My Ears from Lyin' on My Back in My Bed While I Cry Over You—Country Music's Best (and Funniest) Lines.*[31]

As a pastor, I've had my share of times counseling couples—both before and after the wedding. In premarital counseling, I have frequently shared the following stages of a marriage, as described by a husband's reactions to his wife's cold:

> **1st Year:** "Sugar dumpling, I'm worried about you, baby girl. You've got a bad sniffle. I'm putting you in the hospital for a general checkup."
> **2nd Year:** "Listen, honey, go to bed. I've called the doctor to rush over here."
> **3rd Year:** "Better lie down; nothing like a little rest when you feel bad. I'll bring you something to eat."

4th Year: "Look, dear, be sensible; after you feed
the kids, and get the dishes washed, you'd
better lie down for awhile."

5th Year: "Why don't you get up and get yourself
an aspirin? And stop complaining so much!"

6th Year: "If you'd just gargle or something
instead of sitting around and barking in my
face like a seal, I'd appreciate it."

7th Year: "For Pete's sake, stop sneezing. What
are you trying to do, give me pneumonia?!"

(By the way, if you are laughing, *your* marriage may be going downhill too!)

Marital relationships aren't the only things that are full of strife and strain. So are labor and management. So are nations at war. Sadly, it seems as though every newscast carries a story about the inability of human beings to live in positive relationships with other human beings.

I like the story of one fellow who was bragging to some friends, "Yes, there is a proud fighting tradition in my family! My great-great-grandfather stood his ground at Bunker Hill. Then Great-Grandfather valiantly joined up with the troops to destroy the Germans. My grandfather was at Pearl Harbor, and my father fought the North Koreans."

"Mercy!" one of his friends remarked. "Can't your family get along with anyone?"

If you've spent any time around people, you've undoubtedly heard the phrase "You make me sick!" It's an old standard. I know it's only a phrase, but sometimes our emotions in challenging relationships can actually affect our health.

Do people make you sick? Do you feel like life isn't fair when it comes to you and your relationships? Let me give you some very simple steps that will help you in your journey into good relationships.

DON'T CURSE PEOPLE, BLESS THEM!

Bless those who persecute you; bless and do not curse. (Rom. 12:14)

How much can one person bear? "More" would be the answer of Carson McCullers, the novelist who was described at her death as having a "vocation of pain."

"Much of her art," a critic related, "seemed to have flowed from her own tortured life."

Before she was twenty-nine, McCullers had suffered three strokes that paralyzed her left side. Discouraged, she was sure that she could never write again. Eventually, however, she resumed her work, writing a page a day.

Unfortunately, her pain increased in her later years. Her husband committed suicide, and illness left her a virtual cripple. In a rare mention of her troubles, she said, "Sometimes I think God got me mixed up with Job. But Job never cursed God, and neither have I. I carry on."[32]

An act of kindness is the shortest distance between two hearts.

Once while I was watching *Good Morning America,* Jamie Lee Curtis was being interviewed. The interviewer noted that many critics were surprised at her heavy use of profanity in an upcoming movie. Jamie responded, "I can curse like a sailor—a blue streak!" For certain, the world's way is to curse everything in sight. Not me. I want to bless everyone!

An Irish Prayer

May those who love us, love us;
And those that don't love us,
May God turn their hearts;
And if He doesn't turn their hearts,
May He turn their ankles
So we'll know them by their limping.

LOVE EVERYONE, INCLUDING YOURSELF

If you want to be able to love others, you've got to learn to love yourself. Loving God with your whole heart and understanding His love for you provides the foundation that makes it possible to love others. All too often as Christians we fail to see the need to love ourselves, and we fall into the pit of self-degradation and false humility. And that leads to poor self-esteem. It also causes a strain in many of our relationships.

Scripture clearly teaches that we are to love ourselves, or we cannot possibly love our neighbor.

Love is patient, love is kind. It does not envy, it does not boast,
it is not proud. It is not rude, it is not self-seeking, it is not

easily angered, it keeps no record of wrongs. Love does not
delight in evil but rejoices with the truth. It always protects,
always trusts, always hopes, always perseveres. Love never fails.
But where there are prophecies, they will cease; where there are
tongues, they will be stilled; where there is knowledge, it will
pass away. (1 Cor. 13:4–8)

I once heard Denis Waitley say, "The first best-kept secret of total success is that we feel love inside ourselves before we can give it to others." He went on to say, "If there is no sense of value within us, we have nothing to offer to others."

Romans 12:16 says, "Live in harmony with one another." According to Jesus Christ, this is possible only when you "love your neighbor as yourself" (Mark 12:31).

If you don't love yourself, you can't possibly love your neighbor!

A minister friend told me a story some time ago that illustrates beautifully the matter of self-worth in Christian experience. It seems a certain pastor had a very poor self-image. He was a senior pastor, and things were not going well for him in his local church.

Feeling very discouraged, he entered the prayer chapel, knelt at the altar, and prayed a very sad prayer. "O God, I am nothing. I am nothing," he said over and over again.

Just at that time, the associate pastor walked by and was very impressed by the senior pastor's humility. So he joined him in saying, "O Lord, I am nothing … I, too, am nothing."

While both were praying, the church custodian came by the prayer chapel and was moved by the apparent meekness of the leaders of the church. Wanting to share in their experience, he joined them at the altar, and said, "O Lord, I, too, am nothing, nothing, nothing."

The associate pastor paused, looked at the custodian, then turned to the senior pastor and said, "Now look who thinks he's nothing."

A cheerful friend is like a sunny day.

Lee Iacocca once asked legendary football coach Vince Lombardi what it took to make a winning team. The book *Iacocca* records Lombardi's answer:

> There are a lot of coaches with good ball clubs who know the fundamentals and have plenty of discipline but still don't win the game. Then you come to the third ingredient: If you're going to play together as a team, you've got to care for one another. You've got to love each other. Each player has to be thinking about the next guy and saying to himself: "If I don't block that man, Paul is going to get his legs broken. I have to do my job well in order that he can do his." The difference between mediocrity and greatness is the feeling these guys have for each other.[33]

Team sports really do teach us to reach out to one another, and I've tried to use that to my advantage at home with my kids. My son Seth, for example, has always loved baseball. From the time he was eighteen months old, he could swing a small bat and throw a ball. We would often watch the Cincinnati Reds play baseball on television and then go outside and play ball ourselves. Seth really loved to watch Johnny Bench hit home runs!

By the time he reached four years old, I became concerned about his knowledge of the game. Seth always "hit a home run" no matter where the ball went. I can still see him running around our imaginary infield, going into his "Pete Rose slide," taking off his hat, exposing his blond curly locks, and looking up at the pitcher (me), declaring, "Home run, Daddy!"

One afternoon we were in the front yard playing baseball, and I decided it was time to teach Seth that we didn't always hit home runs! First, I launched into a significant lesson on what is means to make an "out." Then I began to explain the purpose of bases. Just about that time I had confused him thoroughly, his mother came out the front door with four of Seth's reading books. I got the idea (it didn't take a rocket scientist!) that the books would serve as bases. Together we carefully placed the books at first, second, third, and home plate. Everything was coming together for a great life lesson.

Then I explained to Seth, "If you overrun a base, and I tag you, you're out."

"Okay, Daddy," he exclaimed, "play ball!"

I pitched a few balls and let Seth run the bases to warm up. Each time he went through the same ritual: headfirst slide into home plate, hat off, dust himself off, and the declaration of "Home run, Daddy!"

The big moment had arrived. I reviewed the rules with a warning: "Seth, if you overrun a base, I'll tag you out."

"Okay, Daddy, play ball."

I reached back for my best pitch. Seth swung mightily and hit the ball toward shortstop. I fielded it beautifully! (Remember, it's a one-man field.) He rounded first, his little legs churning. I called out, "I've got the ball. Don't overrun second base."

He kept going, and I tagged him just before he reached third. "You're out!" I cried in my best umpire's voice.

But Seth kept going. He rounded third and headed for home. Seth went into his patented slide at home plate, got up, took off his baseball cap, dusted his sitter, sat down on home plate, and said, "Home run, Daddy, home run!"

Arriving somewhat out of breath at the scene, I responded. "You're out!"

"Home run!" he said.

"You're out!" I retorted.

"Home run!" he yelled again.

"You're out!" I shot back.

Disgusted, he folded his chubby little arms, shook his curly head and said, "Daddy, it's my books, it's my ball, it's my bat, and if you don't play right, I'm going in the house!"

Now who do you suppose was the one who learned the lesson that day? Sometimes it's better to focus on building up others rather than trying to "improve them." There's an old saying that says:

If you want to lose friends quickly, start bragging about yourself; if you want to make and keep friends, start bragging about others.

—Anonymous

That's pretty good advice. There's no telling how far you can go if you focus your attention on others rather than yourself. I once read a survey by the Wisconsin Restaurant Association that revealed why a restaurant's patrons stopped eating at a certain restaurant. They gave the following reasons:

1 percent	Died
3 percent	Moved away
5 percent	Developed other relationships
9 percent	Preferred a competitor
14 percent	Were dissatisfied about the produce (meal)
68 percent	Felt an attitude of neglect or indifference[34]

You can't show Christ's love to others and demonstrate an attitude of indifference at the same time. It just cannot be done. Romans 12:16 says, "Do not be proud, but be willing to associate with people of low position." Paul continued in Romans 13:9 with an important reminder: "… and whatever other commandment there may be, are summed up in this one rule: 'Love your neighbor as yourself.'"

And of course, these are the words of Jesus Himself: "You have heard that it was said, 'Love your neighbor and hate your enemy.' But I tell you: Love your enemies and pray for those who persecute you, that you may be sons of your Father in heaven. He causes his sun to rise on the evil and the good, and sends rain on the righteous and the unrighteous" (Matt. 5:43–45).

As Christians, we cannot base our ability to love others on anything other than God's love for us. One of my all-time favorite books is *The Jabez Principle* by Harold Ivan Smith. In this insightful book, he said,

> My value comes in God's affirmation of me.
>
> So if people reject me, I still have worth.
>
> So if my mate rejects me, I still have worth.
>
> So if my child rejects me, I still have worth.
>
> So if my employer rejects me, I still have worth.
>
> My worth is not in what I do or say,
>
> in what I acquire or own,
>
> in what I invent or create.
>
> It's in me—a unique person, created by God.[35]

EXAMINE YOUR MOTIVES

"Do not repay anyone evil for evil. Be careful to do what is right in the eyes of everybody" (Rom. 12:17). Taking the high road with everybody is a real challenge! When others make you sick, you should ask yourself the hard question, "Am I at fault? Do I frustrate people to the point of nausea?"

It's been said, "Forgiveness is critical to a Christian's freedom because unforgiveness is the means Satan uses to gain ground in the life of the believer." There is a great story surrounding the painting of *The Last Supper* by Leonardo da Vinci that illustrates this truth. It seems that just before painting the faces of the disciples in his portrayal of the Last Supper, Leonardo had a terrible argument with a fellow artist—so he determined to paint his fellow artist's face into the portrait of Judas Iscariot, and thus take revenge by preserving the man in infamy for succeeding generations. Thus the face of Judas was one of the first he finished, and everyone who looked at it could easily recognize the face of Leonardo's enemy.

However, when he began to paint the face of Christ he couldn't make any progress at all. Something seemed to be frustrating even his best efforts. He finally came to the conclusion that the cause of his difficulty was his bitterness toward his fellow painter. He decided that you cannot at the same time be painting the features of Christ into your own life and painting another with the colors of hatred and enmity. Ultimately, Leonardo chose to forgive in order to create!

The power of forgiveness can be life changing. In the summer of 1994, newspapers and television programs carried the story of Cindy Hartman. While Cindy was living in Conway, Arkansas, her home was burglarized. The burglary happened at night, when Cindy was sleeping peacefully, unaware that a thief had entered her home. The phone rang, and as Cindy prepared to answer the phone, the burglar ripped the phone cord from the wall and ordered Cindy into her closet.

Cindy reported that she instantly fell to her knees and began crying out to God. During her prayer, she paused and asked the would-be thief if she could pray for him. In a state of disbelief, the burglar agreed to the prayer. Cindy began to tell God that she loved this man and forgave him for what he was doing to her.

Cindy Hartman related that the burglar fell to his knees and cried out to God for mercy and forgiveness. The burglar breathed a sigh of relief, got up and went to his car. He promptly unloaded everything he had taken from Cindy's home. Additionally, he unloaded the bullets from his gun and left it with Cindy.

Though frightened, Cindy chose to let God take care of the problem.

It is well to remember that the entire population of the universe, with one trifling exception, is composed of others.
—J. A. Holmes

LEAVE REVENGE TO GOD

"Do not take revenge, my friends, but leave room for God's wrath, for it is written: 'It is mine to avenge; I will repay'" (Rom. 12:19). That's right, give the person who makes you sick over to God!

I once had the marvelous privilege of hearing Victor Frankl speak. Frankl, a German/Jewish doctor who was arrested during World War II by the Gestapo, was placed in prison and thoroughly interrogated by the Nazi secret police under bright lights for hours at a time. They took every one of his possessions, even his wedding band! Frankl said, "I went through many senseless tortures from the hands of the Nazi policemen. I realized that I had only one thing left, the power to choose my own attitude, and I could choose bitterness or forgiveness."

He chose forgiveness! Victor Frankl stands as a wonderful example of leaving revenge to God. Friend, leave revenge to God. He will repay evil for evil!

In our approach to others, we should always do our best to be positive, no matter what kind of history we've experienced with them. Look at the words of one of our greatest presidents. Despite horrible criticism and abuse from others, this was his approach to life:

> *"A drop of honey catches more flies than a gallon of gall." So with men. If you would win a man to your cause, first convince him that you are his sincere friend. Therein is a drop of honey which catches his heart, which, say what he will, is the high road to reason.*
> —Abraham Lincoln

SURROUND THEM WITH LOVE AND PRAYER

The ultimate test of your relationship with the Lord comes when people treat you wrong, when they make you sick, and you begin to pray for them. You may want to start with something like this ...

> Dear God, help me to be willing to honestly look at my own life. Help me to make changes that need to be made. God, help me to accept myself as You have accepted me. Help me to give others the same spirit of love, friendship, and opportunities that You have given me as Your child. For I know as I give them love, offer

them friendship, and take every opportunity to bless them instead of curse them, Your love has the potential to touch their lives and change them for good. May I be Your instrument in touching the very person who makes me so sick. Today I surround them with love and prayers and believe that the end of the problem will be a healthy, loving relationship with them. In Jesus' name, amen.

CHAPTER 10

When the Going Gets Tough, the Tough Get Challenged

Tristan Blann, a seven-year-old cancer patient, always had three stops on Sunday morning at Nashville First Church, where I once pastored.

His first stop was to visit "Mr. Frank," his Sunday school teacher and faithful supplier of candy. His next stop was to visit Uncle "Pek" Gunn, famous poet laureate of Tennessee and purveyor of bubblegum. His final stop was always to see me after the Sunday morning worship service. Invariably he would slap me in the center of the back while I was shaking hands with people, and I'd turn for him to leap into my arms. What a vigorous, enthusiastic, courageous little guy. With a shiny bald head and a million-dollar smile, he'd say, "Hi, Pastor!"

Tristan was the mascot for the 1991 Vanderbilt University basketball team, and you could find him perched on the bench at every game with the head basketball coach, Eddie Folger. He was their number one cheerleader. He understood basketball and was a super little player. In and out of Vanderbilt University Hospital children's unit, Tristan would set up a goal in the courtyard and challenge any visitor to play. He just loved to shoot hoops.

Perhaps his father, Dr. Rob Blann, described him best in this poem:

Shakespeare Would Have Liked My Son

"Cowards die many times before their death
the valiant taste of death but once."
Or at least that's what Shakespeare said.
But my son is valiant.
No one who knows him will deny that.
Yet he has tasted death many times.
He has lived on the poison that tries to kill his cancer.
My valiant son has lived for six more years
Because the doctors were able to poison the poison,
But now they say time has run out.
The chemo just can't work anymore.
One poison is just stronger than the other
And Tristan's many tastes of death
won't keep him much longer from that final one.
Shakespeare's right, you know.
I've just been playing with words
(like he was)
But if you're truly valiant, there is only one death:
so now I have nothing to do
but play with words
and wait for my son's last valiant act.
—Rob Blann, October 29, 1991

On January 16, 1992, my seven-year-old friend, Tristan Blann, went to be with the Lord. Three days later, with the 1,900-seat sanctuary of Nashville First Church full of friends and family, I preached his funeral. What an awesome worship service it was! The Vanderbilt University men's basketball team served as honorary pallbearers. Tributes were offered from around the country. Dale Brown, head coach of the Louisiana State University Tigers, said, "The courage of Tristan Blann was amazing." Larry Woody, sports editor of the *Tennessean*, called Tristan "a valiant little warrior and a hero to his heroes." Tom Norman of the *Nashville Banner* said, "Tristan's positive attitude and courage during his illness were an inspiration to all."

During the service, this poem, written by Tristan's father a few months before his death, was read:

Midnight of Homecoming

*When the house is at its darkest
and silence is so quiet that it screams
and I let myself leave the books to go to bed,
I pause at the children's door—his door actually,
and I watch them in their sleep.
I watch, midnight mad with the moon,
knowing that the little boy
won't be here in a year.
Bewildered with pain and lack of sleep
my mind keeps taking photographs
making memories of what won't be.
Tristan in the top bunk
where I lifted him hours ago
after he had fallen asleep downstairs.
So happy with his homecoming*

So exhausted after the harrowing hospital
and what they did to him there.
And then beautiful Jennifer
lying there like a dream
sleeping in his bottom bunk
forsaking her own room
Staying with him
Because he was afraid to be alone.
Oh, God, stay with us when we are alone.
—Rob Blann, September 19, 1991

Tears streamed down my cheeks. The words, "Oh, God, stay with us when we are alone," caused my mind to reflect back just ten days earlier in Bethany, Oklahoma. I was standing in a cold, windy cemetery with friends Phil and Donna Moore, grieving the loss of their beautiful sixteen-year-old daughter. Asthmatic, but otherwise healthy, Mandy had died quite unexpectedly. It all seemed so unfair to me. But just as Dr. Roger Hahn completed the benediction, I heard a beautiful tenor voice begin to sing.

What a friend we have in Jesus,
All our sins and griefs to bear!

It was the voice of Mandy's father, Phil Moore. Hundreds joined in the singing:

What a privilege to carry everything to God in prayer!
O what peace we often forfeit,

O what needless pain we bear,
All because we do not carry everything to God in prayer.[36]

The words to the song soothed me as I pulled myself together to deliver the funeral message, with three important statements from Deuteronomy 33:27. And now I'd like to share them with you.

ONLY GOD PROVIDES THE ANSWERS TO LIFE

"The eternal God is your refuge, and underneath are the everlasting arms. He will drive out your enemy before you, saying, 'Destroy him!'" (Deut. 33:27). D. R. Davis in his book *The World That We Have Forgotten* said, "Man in his quest for life is a creature of eternity." We are God's creation, and it shows in our hearts! Solomon put it this way in Ecclesiastes 3:11: "He has made everything beautiful in its time. He has also set eternity in the hearts of men."

If God sends stony paths, He provides strong shoes.

You may have heard the story of Helen Keller, the woman who, blind and deaf from infancy, became a noted writer and lecturer. At the age of nine, according to her biography, *The Miracle Worker,* her parents engaged a teacher to establish communication with her. The teacher, Anne Sullivan, took little Helen to the well one day, pumping cold water over Helen's hand and then tapping on her palm. Helen miraculously began to learn communication skills.

Often left untold is the fact that Helen Keller's parents were deeply devoted Christians who desperately wanted her to know about God. The Kellers contacted the great preacher Phillips Brook and asked him to tutor Helen in the faith. Dr. Brooks reported, "Though she had never heard a word from the outside world about a Supreme Being, she responded, 'I have been wishing for quite awhile that someone would teach me about Him. For I have been thinking about Him for a long time.'" God had put the desire for the eternal deep within her heart. John reminded us that He is "the true light that gives light to every man" (John 1:9).

My greatest comfort while facing the deaths of Tristan and Mandy was knowing that they embraced the reality of John 3:16: "For God so loved the world that he gave his one and only Son, that whoever believes in him shall not perish but have eternal life."

Facing tragedy is no easy task. It sometimes forces you to look into the face of your fears. In his book *The Superman Syndrome,* Jack Kuhatschek wrote, "I am afraid of heights. I have been known to crawl on my hands and knees to the edge of a high balcony in order to look down. Imagine, then, how I felt when a camp director told me I had to rappel down the side of a steep cliff.

"'Everybody does it,' he said matter-of-factly. 'It's part of our program.'

"With sweaty palms and pounding heart, I eased backward off the edge of the cliff, supported by a rope and a safety line. In order to walk down the face of the cliff, I was told to keep my body perpendicular to the cliff. Every nerve and fiber screamed at me to straighten up, to get in a vertical rather than a horizontal position. Yet those who did so lost their footing and were left dangling high above the ground. Only by fighting my natural urges, and by trusting the ropes and those who held them, did I manage to make it safely to the bottom. What a relief!

"That fearful experience of rappelling has become a parable of faith to me. There have been many times in my life when God has asked me to ease over the edge of a cliff, to trust Him for something that seemed unsafe and frightening. The primary difference, of course, is that both the safety rope and the person at the top of the cliff are invisible—while the cliff and its dangers are in plain sight!"[37]

ONLY GOD PROVIDES THE ANSWERS TO DEATH

Moses was facing death when he said, "The eternal God is your refuge." Death is inevitable. It is no respecter of persons. It is one of those fixed decrees of an unchanging God. It visits the rich and the poor, the sick and the healthy. No one is exempt! Visit the cemeteries of your city, and you will find all age groups represented there. As a pastor, I have stood by the graveside of a stillborn child, and I have been there when an aged saint went home to be with Jesus. James said, "You are a mist that appears for a little while and then vanishes" (James 4:14). How true.

We all must face death. I like the words of the songwriter who said,

> *While I draw this fleeting breath,*
> *When my eyes shall close in death,*
> *When I rise to worlds unknown,*
> *And behold Thee on Thy throne,*
> *Rock of Ages, cleft for me,*
> *Let me hide myself in Thee.*[38]
> —Augustus M. Toplady

Outside of God's refuge, the world is an empty, lonely, cold place to live. This is especially true for those who do not know Christ when they come to the hour of death.

In 1 Corinthians 15:56, Paul said, "The sting of death is sin, and the power of sin is the law." He went on to preach a resurrection message, saying:

1. Death is a passage.
2. Death is not the end.
3. Death is a new beginning.

We *can* face physical death with resurrection life!

When Moses was facing death, he said, "And underneath are the everlasting arms." He made this statement of affirmation based on personal experience. He had known the extremes of wealth and poverty. He had known joy and sorrow. Through every crisis in his life, Moses knew that God had provided answers. Now facing death, Moses knew that he would not have to cross death's chilling Jordan River alone. The strength and inner confidence that Moses verbalized in Deuteronomy 33:27 are reflected in the words of Tristan's mother just six days before he went to heaven.

I sit here in the darkened, quiet room, watching my son suffer silently. For six years he has battled valiantly against the cancer which is even now overtaking his brain. He doesn't cry or even ask why he should have to endure this, but spends his time endlessly telling us how much he loves everyone. As he approaches death, his main topic of conversation is love; his concern for others is now the controlling thought in his ever-dwindling

"awake times." Jesus commanded us to love one another as I have loved you—by this shall all men know ye are my disciples (John 13:34–35). Lord, thank You for teaching me discipleship through my child.
—Barbara Blann, January 10, 1992

Life is tough, but God never fails to provide the assistance to see us through the most painful moments.

Ultimate hope:
That God is there,
That God does care,
That God can cope.
—June Bingham

That is our assurance!

CHAPTER 11

I've Gone to Look for Myself. If I Return Before I Get Back, Ask Me to Wait

Robb Robinson, a Tennessee state senator and funeral director, has frequently shared humorous stories with me. One such story took place in Nashville.

After officiating at a funeral, a local minister took the customary lead-car position in the procession to the cemetery. It was during the Christmas season, and the pastor became preoccupied with thoughts of the gifts he needed to purchase after the graveside services. As he approached the Spring Hill Cemetery, he looked left and saw the K-Mart store conveniently located across the street. Obviously lost in deep thought, he turned left into K-Mart parking lot instead of making the required right turn into the cemetery. As he drove through the parking lot looking for a parking space, he happened to look in his rearview mirror, and he saw a string of cars following, all with lights on!

Now that's what I call getting *lost* in deep thought! That pastor could have been the one who anonymously sent me the following message on my fax machine one day: "I've Gone to Look for Myself. If I Return Before I Get Back, Ask Me to Wait." Those are words just begging to be put into a book!

When it comes to being lost (or at a loss), there's no place where I feel it more than on the golf course. That's been true for many years. Years ago, I was privileged to serve as John Maxwell's first pastoral staff member at Faith Memorial Church in Lancaster, Ohio. John, a noted author, lecturer, and former senior pastor of Skyline Wesleyan Church, has been my mentor for several decades. He has guided me in matters of leadership, preaching, evangelism, and church growth. And from time to time, John, who is an excellent golfer, has felt the need to mentor me in the great game of golf!

On one rainy fall day many years ago back in Lancaster, I was busy working on a project when the intercom buzzer sounded. "Toler," the booming voice of Maxwell said, "let's play eighteen!"

What a welcome diversion! I thought to myself. In a matter of minutes we loaded our golf clubs into John's 1972 Ford Pinto and hurried to the nearby Carrollwood golf course. Since it was raining steadily, the course was not crowded, and we were able to tee off immediately.

For the first five holes, it appeared that the Maxwell Mentoring Course on golf was working. "What a great game—thanks for asking me to come along," I said to John.

As we approached the sixth tee box, I courageously asked John to lend me his three wood. He was proud of his new clubs and most willing to share them with his prized pupil. I stepped up to the tee box and took a practice swing. Feeling ready, I swung mightily at the little white ball.

To this day, I don't remember whether I actually hit that ball, but what I do remember is the club slipping out of my hands and sailing twenty feet into the air! Embarrassing? You bet! And if that wasn't humbling enough, the three wood landed in a pine tree! Maxwell was in a state of utter disbelief.

"You just threw my new club into a tree!" he cried. "How on earth are we going to get it down?"

Mustering all the confidence I had, I said, "Give me your shoe." Obediently, John sat down on the cart and handed me his golf shoe. I carefully aimed his shoe at the club and gave it a mighty heave, expecting to knock the club out of the pine tree. To my dismay, his shoe got stuck in the same tree!

Undaunted, I said, "Give me your other shoe." Again, without arguing, John handed his other shoe to me. Taking better aim, I tossed his shoe at the club, and missed again! Can you believe it? The second shoe stayed in the tree, also.

As the drizzle started to become a downpour, John stood up and said, "Toler, you big dummy! No, wait a minute—I'm the dummy! Stan, give me your shoe!"

In a spirit of cooperation—and fear—I took off my shoe and handed it to him. And why not? He had a three wood and two golf shoes in that pine tree! Taking careful aim, John threw my shoe at the club. Up it went, approximately eighteen feet in the air, and missed everything. Feeling more confident, I picked up my shoe and tossed it at the club. It missed the club completely, but as it fell downward, it knocked one of John's shoes loose. But in the process, my shoe got stuck in the tree! John immediately grabbed his shoe that had fallen to the ground, and clutched it defensively. Now neither of us had a complete pair of shoes, and still the golf club was stuck in the tree.

By this time, several other golfers had passed the sixth tee, observing this Laurel and Hardy comedy routine. Remarkably, most did not speak or offer to help us. (Can you blame them?)

When every effort had failed in retrieving the golf club, my esteemed friend finally climbed the huge pine tree and personally retrieved the club and our shoes. At that point, it began to thunder, and the rain was coming down even harder. The only thing left to do was quit for the day and go to the clubhouse for hot chocolate.

Feeling embarrassed and helpless, we drove rapidly across the course to the clubhouse. As John opened the door, the room became silent. And that's when paranoia instantly gripped us. Sure enough—the other golfers had told on us! As we stood in the doorway, laughter erupted like you've never heard.

We shut the door, turned right around, and went straight home. And believe me, it was a long time before we played golf there again.

Doesn't life just seem to go that way sometimes? We often get lost and cannot find our way. And the whole world seems to laugh at our best efforts. We feel so scared and unable to cope. Guidance from God is what we need in those situations. But how do we find such guidance?

Dr. James Dobson recently stated on his Focus on the Family radio broadcast, "There are few topics filled with as much confusion and contradiction as the subject of God's guidance." Many people view guidance from God in the same manner as the young man who tried to decide which young lady he should date. He began to pray to God for guidance in the matter. In his prayer, he said, "God, I'll flip a coin. You direct it. Heads it's Patty and tails it's Beatrice." He flipped his quarter and looked at it and saw that it was tails. He quickly prayed, "Okay, God, how about two out of three!"

Finding guidance from God is a greater process than flipping a coin or closing your eyes and pointing at random to a spot in your Bible.

COMMIT YOUR PLANS TO GOD

Your word is a lamp to my feet and a light for my path. (Ps. 119:105)

One of the most exciting aspects of our spiritual walk is realizing that God has a plan for each of His children. He has not left us to wander in the darkness of indecision.

Solomon was very specific about the process of planning in Proverbs 16:1: "To man belong the plans of the heart, but from the LORD comes the reply of the tongue." The message is clear. We may have our plans, but God wants to unfold His plans for our lives. "In his heart a man plans his course, but the LORD determines his steps" (Prov. 16:9).

The only ability God asks for is availability.

Proverbs 16:3 tells us, "Commit to the LORD whatever you do, and your plans will succeed." What are we to commit? First, we are to commit our lives to Christ. Paul said of the Macedonians, "They gave themselves first to the Lord" (2 Cor. 8:5).

Second, we are to commit our service to the Lord. God is interested in the work of our hands, regardless of whether it takes place in Christian ministry, domestic situations, or the marketplace. "His intent was that now, through the church, the manifold wisdom of God should be made known to the rulers and authorities in the heavenly realms" (Eph. 3:10). Before God shaped the world, He worked out the plan of servanthood.

> *I know not the way God leads me, but well do I know my Guide.*
> —Martin Luther

COMMIT YOUR ABILITIES TO GOD

One of the things many people don't realize is that the word *commitment* also involves faith. It is a frightening matter to talk about committing your abilities to God. We live in a time when few real commitments seem to be made. In *Point Man,* Steve Farrar said, "Commitment is cheap in marriage, business, politics, and even athletics. Commitment is cheap in professional sports when a running back will sign a six-year multimillion-dollar contact and then stay out of training camp on his third year because the team won't renegotiate his contract. Why does he want to renegotiate? Because some other backs in the league recently signed new contracts worth more than his. He refuses to keep his commitment, until he gets his way. One player recently hinted that if his contract wasn't renegotiated, he wouldn't be able to give 100 percent on the field."[39]

You have been gifted by God to do His work. Doing service for God requires hard work and a definite commitment for life! There must never be a letup in your spiritual walk with God.

Whenever you are seeking guidance from God, do not overlook your own gifts. God has given every believer at least one spiritual gift; therefore, when God calls on you to do something, you will be capable! He will not fail you in this point! You may be frightened by the opportunity, but God will energize your abilities. As it says in Romans 11:29, "God's gifts and his call are irrevocable."

Following through with what God has assigned to us can be scary. We are often like the little girl who was afraid to go to bed in the dark by herself. After three or four trips to her parents' bedroom, her father sought to reassure her.

"Look, honey," he said, "you are not really alone in your bedroom. God is watching over you. God is everywhere, and He is in your bedroom, too."

The little girl was not reassured by this. She started back to her room but stopped at the door and said in a loud whisper, "God, if You are in there, please don't say anything. It would scare me to death."

Stepping forward really does take faith. I remember an experience at a small frame church in Baileysville, West Virginia, that really tested my faith when I was a boy. A revival meeting was held, and the Toler family attended every service. I was just a seven-year-old boy at the time, but one night I went to the altar to pray. Clearly and forcefully, I felt the call of God to preach. Was I frightened? Yes! It took me seven years to get the courage to tell another human being of God's call on my life. Thankfully by then, though, I knew that God had gifted me to preach the gospel. Ultimately, at age fourteen, I committed my abilities to God, sought His guidance, and surrendered to Him and His calling.

If you have doubts, remember these words:

*God looks at you and sees a beautiful person waiting to be born! If you
could see in a vision the man God meant you to be, never again could
you be quiet. You rise up and try and succeed. They tell us that ants are
born with wings and use them, know the glory and flame and rapture of
flight, then tear these wings off deliberately, choosing to live their lives out
as crawling insects. Choosing that when God gave them the vast empire
of the air! Don't make the same mistake by selling yourself short!*
—Dr. Norman Vincent Peale

And don't forget the words of the apostle Paul:

*Brothers, think of what you were when you were called. Not
many of you were wise by human standards; not many were
influential; not many were of noble birth. But God chose the
foolish things of the world to shame the wise; God chose the
weak things of the world to shame the strong. (1 Cor. 1:26–27)*

COMMIT YOUR MINISTRY TO GOD

It takes resolve to do the will of God. Jesus said, "Not everyone who
says to me, 'Lord, Lord' will enter the kingdom of heaven, but only
he who does the will of my Father who is in heaven" (Matt. 7:21).

When I was a junior in high school, I pastored my first church.
That caused me a great deal of pain and persecution. I was often
called "Jesus freak" and "holy boy." On one occasion a student filled
up the sink with water in the boys' restroom and said to me, "Come
on, preacher boy, walk on water!" But that didn't faze me, because
I had resolved to follow Christ and preach His Word. Perhaps

the words of a song written by my brother Terry best describe my commitment:

I Will Live My Life for Christ

(Chorus)
I will live my life for Christ
For me He paid such a price
My ambitions and plans are all in His hands
I will live my life for Christ

(Verse 1)
You may spend your life seeking pleasure
Or filling your pockets with treasure
Living for yourself, loving no one else
Living with no thought of forever.

(Verse 2)
I once lived my life that way
Then Jesus spoke sweet peace, one happy day.
He made such a change, I praise His name
For He took all my sins away.[40]

Confidence in Christ is at the heart of our ability to act on the calling we receive. General William Booth, founder of the Salvation Army, was once asked, "What is the secret of your success?"

Booth responded, "From the day I got the poor of London on my heart and a vision of what Jesus Christ would do for them, I made up my mind that God should have all of William Booth there was; and if anything has been achieved, it is because God has had all the adoration of my heart, all the power of my will and all the influence of my life."

What a model that is for all who minister in Jesus' name! God wants 100 percent of you now!

STEPS TO UNDERSTANDING GOD'S GUIDANCE

In *God's Guidance: A Slow and Certain Light*, Elisabeth Elliot told of two adventurers who stopped by to see her, all loaded with equipment for traveling through the rain forest east of the Andes. They sought no advice, just a few phrases with which to converse with the Indians.

She wrote, "Sometimes we come to God as the two adventurers came to me—confident and, we think, well-informed and well-equipped. But it has occurred to us that with all our accumulation of stuff, something is missing."

Elliot insisted that we often ask God for too little. We know what we need: a yes or no answer, please, to a simple question. Or perhaps a road sign. Something quick and easy to point the way.

She continued, "What we really ought to have is the Guide Himself. Maps, road signs, and a few useful phrases are good things, but infinitely better is Someone who has been there before and knows the way."[41]

A Blueprint for Achievement

BELIEVE while others are doubting.
PLAN while others are playing.

STUDY while others are sleeping.
DECIDE while others are delaying.
PREPARE while others are daydreaming.
BEGIN while others are procrastinating.
WORK while others are wishing.
SAVE while others are wasting.
LISTEN while others are talking.
SMILE while others are talking.
COMMEND while others are criticizing.
PERSIST while others are quitting.

Step One: Be Ready When God Calls!

My college president and hero in the faith, Dr. Melvin Maxwell, used to say, "We must be minutemen for the Lord." My personal formula for seeking God's guidance has always been to pray, read God's Word, listen for His call, and go where He calls at a moment's notice!

If you haven't already guessed, Dr. Melvin Maxwell is the father of my friend John Maxwell, who said,

Ordinary people who make simple, spiritual commitments under the
lordship of Christ make an extraordinary impact on their world.
—John Maxwell

Step Two: Be Sure It's God Calling!

I've often prayed, "God, if this is You, I'm willing and ready, but if this feeling is a direct result of too much pepperoni pizza, then grant me the wisdom to go take an antacid and get over it!"

Some years ago, I was invited to speak in Oshkosh, Nebraska. I agreed to go before I had the opportunity to talk with a travel agent. What a big mistake!

As the time of the speaking engagement approached, my secretary began to work on my travel plans. Frustrated, she came into my office, complaining, "You can't get there from here!" And she was right! Traveling from Washington Court House, Ohio, to Oshkosh, Nebraska, was impossible. Immediately I picked up the phone and called the conference coordinator to tell him it would involve six plane changes, an overnight stay in Chicago, and lots of money!

Undaunted, he said, "Come on out! Everyone has difficulty getting to Oshkosh!"

When the day finally arrived for me to go, as planned, I spent the night in Chicago, made a total of six stops and eventually landed in North Platte, Nebraska. A lovely pastoral couple met me at the airport, loaded me into their little Chevette Scooter, and then began the trip to Oshkosh—a two-and-one-half-hour drive. Spending that amount of time jam-packed in a Chevette Scooter causes me even now to pause and thank God that Chevrolet quit making those cars!

After the luggage surrounding me was removed, I unfolded my five-foot-eight frame and climbed out of the car. Greeted warmly by everyone, I walked toward the little white-frame church building. As I entered the front door, I noticed a sign that said, "There's no other place anywhere near this place like this place—this must be the place!" Naturally, I laughed heartily after all I had gone through to get there!

I have to say, God really spoke to me through that sign on the church door. The message was crystal clear: God's place of service is the best place in the world! With so much dissatisfaction in our world, we must learn to be content with our place of ministry.

Having served in churches in several states over nearly thirty years of ministry, I can tell you that I have applied the words of the great apostle Paul to each place of service. Paul said, "I have learned to be content whatever the circumstances" (Phil. 4:11). He continued in verses 12 and 13, "I know what it is to be in need, and I know what it is to have plenty. I have learned the secret of being content in any and every situation, whether well fed or hungry, whether living in plenty or in want. I can do everything through him who gives me strength."

So many people believe that the grass is greener on the other side and often try to get to the other side. Sometimes, though, the grass just *looks* greener because it's filled with poison ivy. I think, however, that Erma Bombeck, the great "folk theologian," had it right when she said, "The grass is always greener over the septic tank!" That's especially true when you are living outside the will of God.

When you are sure of God's calling and you are obedient, it's reassuring. My value, my self-esteem, and my happiness are all found with my being in "God's place"!

Step Three: Clarify the Guidance

When you think you hear God speaking to you, be sure about it. Is it yes? Is it no? Should I get help quick? Can I find scriptural backing or is this totally contrary to His Word? God will never tell you to do anything wrong!

To emphasize the importance of being clear about God's guidance, let me tell you a story about a junior high Sunday school teacher. One Sunday in class, he was trying to illustrate the word *miracle*.

"Boys and girls," he said, "suppose I stood on the roof of a ten-story building, lost my balance, and fell off. Then all of a sudden, in midair, a whirlwind swept me up and brought me safely to the ground. Now what word would you use to describe this?"

After a long silence a boy raised his hand and asked, "Luck?"

"True, true," replied the teacher. "It could be luck. But that's not the word I wanted. I'll repeat the story. There I am on top of the ten-story building again, and I fall. A whirlwind catches me in midair and places me safely on the ground. Think now, what word would describe the situation?"

"Accident," cried out one girl.

"No, no," answered the teacher. "Listen carefully for the third time. I'm on that same building, I fall and am swept to safety by a sudden whirlwind. What word could account for my safely reaching the ground?"

The boys and girls shouted in unison: "Practice!"

When it comes to knowing God's guidance, you can't rely on luck or accidents. You have to look to Scripture. As Paul said, "All Scripture is God-breathed and is useful for teaching, rebuking, correcting and training in righteousness, so that the man of God may be thoroughly equipped for every good work" (2 Tim. 3:16–17).

Step Four: Obey the Message

If God tells you to do it, by all means do what He says—or you will be sorry. If we try to wrestle with God over who's in charge, we will regret it. We'll be like the captain of a large ship who saw the lights of what looked like another ship off in the distance one foggy night while he was standing on the bridge of his vessel. As he progressed, he realized the other ship was on a collision course with his, so he quickly signaled to the approaching ship, "Please change your course ten degrees west."

The reply returned back, blinking through the fog: "You change your course ten degrees east."

The captain became furious and shot a message back to the other ship, "I'm a sea captain with thirty-five years' experience. You change your course ten degrees west!"

Without hesitation, the signal flashed back, "I'm a seaman fourth class. You change your course ten degrees east!"

Enraged and incensed, the captain knew that he was heading for a terrible head-on crash. He blazed a last message to the fast-approaching ship: "I'm a fifty-thousand-ton freighter. You change your course ten degrees west!"

The simple message winked back. "I'm a lighthouse. You change …"[42]

Life is fragile. Handle with prayer.

It's not always easy to discover what message God is trying to give us. Recently, I developed a newfound friendship with Dwight "Ike" Reighard, a Southern Baptist pastor from Georgia. While eating in one of Fayetteville's "meat and three" restaurants, Ike began to share about the loss of both his wife and baby due to a pregnancy complication.

Recovering from grief, he discovered, is like climbing a ladder one rung at a time. At first he asked, "Why?" Then he asked, "Why me?" Finally, after much prayer and help from a Christian counselor, he came to the conclusion that while he did not understand why they died, he needed to focus on the *what* instead of the *why*. He asked, "God, what message of guidance do You have for me?" Ike then began to acknowledge his needs and fill them with God's guidance.

Faith plus patience equals hope.

Step Five: Give Thanks to God for the Call

> *His divine power has given us everything we need for life and godliness through our knowledge of him who called us by his own glory and goodness. (2 Peter 1:3)*

God really does provide everything we need, whether we recognize it or not. Joyce Hollyday stated in an article for *Sojourners:*

> A hazard of communities and people with a vocation to seek the kingdom of God and to work for justice is to forget to celebrate what we have, as well as what we haven't. We see what we have not accomplished, what is wrong, and what we lack, but it is more awkward for us to give thanksgiving and praise. We may fear being accused of being naïve. Often those who are materially poor have attitudes of praise which markedly affect their lives. Little children's prayers are almost exclusively prayers of thanksgiving. In the gospel, faith and praise are intimately linked.[43]

She is right. Receiving guidance from God involves a simple, childlike faith. Therefore, our response to God's call must always include thanksgiving and praise.

Too many believers fail to give thanks when God calls. It is important to give thanks, because we are told to do so in the Word of God. Furthermore, if we have experienced the indwelling of the Holy Spirit, we will consistently thank God for all things.

It is my firm belief that when we fail to give thanks to God for His call, we step out of His will for our lives. In 2 Timothy 3:1–2, Paul warned his student Timothy, "But mark this: There will be terrible times in the last days. People will be lovers of themselves, lovers of money, boastful, proud, abusive, disobedient to their parents, ungrateful, unholy." With this in mind, we should never offer prayers to God without offering words of thanksgiving and praise.

Why should we give thanks? Because it is our entrance into God's throne room. Norman Vincent Peale coined the phrase *thanks-living*. I believe thanks-living was practiced by the early Christians and must become a daily ritual in the lives of twenty-first-century believers.

Always thank God for His guidance, even when you don't particularly like it! God knows what's best for you.

To know the will of God is our greatest knowledge. To
do the will of God is our greatest achievement.
—George Truett

CHAPTER 12

Life's Adventure in Wonderland

*Unless you change and become like little children, you will
never enter the kingdom of heaven. (Matt. 18:3)*

I'll never forget the time our family moved from West Virginia to
Ohio and all the changes that we experienced. Not only did we have
indoor plumbing for the first time, but instead of having a coal stove
for cooking, we had a gas stove with an oven. That was quite a change
for my mother.

We hadn't been in Ohio long when Mother excitedly went to the
grocery store and purchased a canned ham. She read the instructions,
preheated the oven to 425 degrees, and placed the canned ham in
the oven … can and all! Mom smiled sweetly and said, "Off we go to
church; our ham will be ready when we get back!"

After church we hurried home, looking forward to eating our
oven-roasted ham. But to our dismay, we discovered our canned
ham was just a bit "overcooked." It had exploded in the oven, blown
off the oven door, and sent most of the ham to the ceiling! Change
surely is difficult, even for mothers!

The dictionary defines *change* as "putting something in place of something else." In other words, change is the process of alteration and replacement.

Today our world is changing at a frightening pace. If you look back two centuries, people lived in quite a different manner. Here's how a newspaper columnist described the America of more than two hundred years ago: "Life expectancy was thirty-eight years; the average workweek was seventy-two hours; and the median annual wage was $300.00. On occasion, epidemics claimed the lives of entire families. Rivers carried cholera, typhoid, and yellow fever, and one of these diseases killed one out of five residents of Philadelphia in 1793."[44]

Change is never easy. Friends who are seniors have told me that when trains were first introduced, many naysayers predicted that passengers would get nosebleeds because the trains were traveling at the speed of fifteen miles per hour. Additionally, real concern was expressed that travelers might suffocate when going through tunnels.

Even the birth of the telephone was an exasperating experience for business leaders. For example, Joshua Coppersmith was arrested in Boston for attempting to sell stock in a company that would design and build telephones. His arrest was based on the fact that "well-informed people know it is impossible to transmit the human voice over a wire."

Are you struggling with all the changes taking place in the world today? Is the whole process frightening to you? Well, get ready—more changes are ahead for you!

> Not in the lifetime of most men has there been so much
> grave and deep apprehension....

The domestic economic situation is in chaos.

Our dollar is weak throughout the world. Prices are so
high as to be utterly impossible. Of our troubles man
can see no end.

—*Harper's Weekly,* 1857

The 1990 United States Census revealed that even more startling
changes have occurred. For example, one hundred years ago, 50 percent
of the labor force was in agriculture and only 2 percent was in information, communication, and publication. Today, the reverse is true!

Not only has *what* people do changed, but so have the *hows* to
do it. According to *Harper's Index,* the average American will hold
eight different jobs and live in more than thirty different houses during his or her lifetime.

In his book *Trigger Points,* Michael Kami used Coca-Cola as an
illustration of rapid change. Several years ago Coca-Cola sold two
kinds of drinks, Coca-Cola and Tab. Today, the same company mar-
kets Coca-Cola Classic, Diet Coke, Caffeine-Free Coke, Caffeine-Free
Diet Coke, Cherry Coke, Diet Cherry Coke, and many more.

That's quite a change from Henry Ford's philosophy about his
favorite product: "You can have a car any color you want as long as
it's black!" I believe future generations will look back on the turn of
the century as a time of great change.

Probably the best example of change, though, is McDonald's. Hardly
a two-week period passes without something new or different going on at
McDonald's: a new product, an incredible offer, a new game, a new gift.
"We can invent," Ray Kroc once said, "faster than the others can copy."[45]

But it doesn't stop with Coca-Cola or McDonald's. Change touches on almost every aspect of life. While change is not always welcomed, it does not always have to be a bad experience. Some change is good.

In the January 1994 issue of *McCall's* magazine, Dr. Judith Sills listed these eight amusing signs that indicate you might need to make some changes:

1. The counter boy at Dunkin' Donuts greets you by name.
2. Dust balls fall out when you unroll your exercise mat.
3. On Monday you start wishing for Friday.
4. You often lose patience with your children and your coworkers.
5. It has been two years since you tried a new cologne.
6. You keep saying you'll sign up for stenciling lessons but never do.
7. All you seem to do on Saturdays is run errands.
8. A sunset doesn't take your breath away.[46]

During my college days, the book *I'm OK, You're OK* was required reading. Tom Harris, the famous psychiatrist who wrote this enormously successful book, said there are three reasons people change. The first is that people change when it is more painful to remain as they are. For example, perhaps you are in a job that is very painful to you. You cannot imagine being in that job for the rest of your life, so you make a change because it is more painful to stay where you are than to change.

A second time for change, according to Harris, is when we find ourselves at the point of despair. Perhaps we suddenly come to the realization that we are about to lose our marriage, our job, our health. At that point we may change. You have probably heard people say, "I had to reach rock bottom before I could take hold of my life." When they say that, what they're really experiencing is despair.

Harris believed that there is a third motive for change. He called it the "Eureka Stage." That is, some people change because they discover— much to their surprise—that there is something better that they have been missing. Of course, this is the message of the gospel. There is a richer, fuller life that is available to anyone who will receive it.[47]

Genesis 32 records an incident in the life of Jacob that beautifully illustrates the positive aspects of change. The truth is that if we are honest, all of us would change something about ourselves.

The Scripture says, "So Jacob was left alone, and a man wrestled with him till daybreak. When the man saw that he could not overpower him, he touched the socket of Jacob's hip so that his hip was wrenched as he wrestled with the man" (Gen. 32:24–25). The Bible gives us a view from God's perspective. Someone has said, "He doesn't change us so that He can accept us. He accepts us so that He can change us!"

In the end, it is important to remember that we cannot become what we need to be by remaining what we are.[48]

—Max De Pree

As a young kid, I enjoyed big-time TV wrestling. Some of my favorite wrestlers were Dusty Roads, The Sheik, and Cocoa Brazil. On Saturday afternoon, my brothers and I gathered around the

black-and-white TV set and watched wrestling. During the TV com-
mercials, we often stripped down to our boxer shorts and practiced
our own wrestling skills. Being the older, stronger brother, I usually
won the match. If my brother Terry ended up on the bottom of the
pile, our little brother, Mark, jumped on top of me, and the fight was
on! We'd battle until someone yelled, "Uncle!"

I'll never forget one Saturday after the "fights," I was especially
energized by the television match. During the commercial break, I
picked Terry up and threw him across the room. There was silence.
Terry was not breathing!

He's dead! I thought. I fell to my knees and cried out to God for
forgiveness. I began to weep and cry aloud, "Oh, Terry, forgive me.
I'm going to jail, I didn't mean to kill my brother."

Suddenly, Terry rolled over, began laughing and pounding the
floor with enthusiasm. "I tricked you! I fooled you!" he shouted.
Well, the fight was really on again in only a matter of seconds.

"Uncle!" he yelled. It's a good thing, too, because I think I had
murder in my heart!

In the Bible, Jacob was a swindler, a cheat, and a manipulator.
But he was changed through a wrestling match with an angel. As
God dealt with Jacob in this one-on-one match, Jacob caught a
glimpse of what his life could become through change. And change
he did.

CHANGED THROUGH A CRISIS

What are you wrestling with this week? Shad Helmstetter, in his
book *You Can Excel in Times of Change*, discussed the major changes
we face in life. He focused on matters of loss, separation, health,

relationships, and personal growth. Then he enumerated the following steps for dealing with the matter of change:

1. Recognize and understand the change you are going through.
2. Accept or reject the change. That is, decide how you are going to let the change affect you.
3. Choose your attitude toward this change. We cannot always choose the changes, but we can always choose our attitude toward the change.
4. Choose your style of handling the change. Will you use acquiescence, active resistance, or positive acceleration?
5. Choose your action. Set out a strategy for dealing with this change.
6. Review, evaluate, and adjust as you go along.[49]

Of course, not everyone accepts the need for change gracefully. In a *Peanuts* comic strip I once saw, Lucy is walking along the road with Charlie Brown, who asks her, "Lucy, are you going to make any New Year's resolutions?"

Lucy hollers back at him, knocking him off his feet: "What? What for? What's wrong with me now? I like myself the way I am! Why should I change? What in the world is the matter with you, Charlie Brown? I'm all right the way I am! I don't have to improve. How could I improve? How, I ask you? How?"[50]

Everyone thinks of changing the world, but
no one thinks of changing himself.
—Leo Tolstoy

CHANGED THROUGH PERSISTENCE

Then the man said, "Let me go, for it is daybreak." But Jacob
replied, "I will not let you go unless you bless me." (Gen. 32:26)

Have you ever noticed how God often waits to resolve a problem to
see if we really mean business? Have you ever looked up to God and
said, "God, if You'll get me out of this mess, I promise I'll change"?
In the case of Jacob, he was finished being a spiritual sprinter! He
was ready to make a commitment to worship the true and living
God. He was essentially saying, "I won't cry 'uncle!' until You bless
me!" In this day of instant grits, instant coffee, and microwave
popcorn, we must remember that spiritual worship does not come
without prayer, fasting, and agonizing before God.

Sometimes I think we've lost our ability to persevere before God.
Harold Sherman wrote a book titled *How to Turn Failure Into Success.*
In it, he gave the following code of persistence:

1. I will never give up so long as I know I am
   right. I will believe that all things will work
   out for me if I hang on to the end.
2. I will be courageous and undismayed in the
   face of odds.

3. I will not permit anyone to intimidate or deter me from my goals.

4. I will fight to overcome all physical handicaps and setbacks.

5. I will try again and again and yet again to accomplish what I desire.

6. I will take new faith and resolution from the knowledge that all successful men and women have had to fight defeat and adversity.

7. I will never surrender to discouragement or despair no matter what seeming obstacles may confront me.[51]

Before Jacob determined to be persistent, I think he had to wrestle with the decision to commit himself to real-life priorities. That can be tough. Some people make decisions like the family in a story I especially enjoy. It seems the family decided to leave the city and move to the country. They bought a ranch and made plans to raise cattle. They completed the relocation process and set about building their ranch. About six months later, friends came to see them. They wanted to see the ranch and the cattle. The friend said to the owner of the ranch, "What do you call the ranch?" The owner of the ranch said, "I wanted to call it the *Flying W.* My wife wanted to name it the *Suzie Q.* But my oldest son wanted to call it the *Bar J*, and my youngest son wanted to call it the *Lazy Y Ranch.*"

"So," he said, "what *did* you name it?"

"Well, we named it the *Flying W, Suzie Q, Bar J, Lazy Y Ranch,*" he said.

"Okay," the friend said, "but where are the cattle?"

The owner said, "Well, we don't have any. None of them survived the branding."

If cattle cannot survive the branding of misplaced priorities, then neither can you. If you can't decide what's important, you're just going to be wounded, beaten up, bruised, battle-scarred, defeated, and discouraged most of the time. When you get your priorities in order, you will cry out, "God, does my life please You?"

When Jacob said, "I will not let you go," he was ready to put God first in his life, even if it cost him everything. Jacob paused to worship God in a time of unparalleled crisis. He was willing to let God change him.

You can change too! It doesn't matter whether you are poor, physically limited, filled with hatred, or manipulative—you don't have to stay bound and oppressed by Satan. You are God's child. He will help you break the chains of sin and overcome the Enemy! Satan will be the one who cries "uncle"!

You are the way you are because that's the way you want to be. If you really wanted to be different, you would be in the process of changing right now.

—Fred Smith

CHANGED THROUGH CONFESSION

"The man asked him, 'What is your name?' 'Jacob,' he answered" (Gen. 32:27). I've often wondered why the angel asked Jacob his name. The name *Jacob* means "heel catcher" or "deceiver." It is my personal belief that he answered "Jacob" in order to confess his sinfulness as a person. If you were to confess your own character flaws, what would they be? Tough question? You bet! Right now there's a big-time wrestling match going on for your soul! When you confess your weaknesses to God, you are on your way to spiritual victory!

Martin Luther, the great leader of the Reformation, was in his study one day preparing to preach when, he wrote, "Satan came into my study." He continued:

> While I was seated at my desk studying the Word of God, Satan walked into the room with a huge scroll under his arm. He stopped me in the middle of my studies and said, "Martin Luther, listed on this scroll are all the sins that you've ever committed. Read your sins. Martin Luther, read them!"

> Satan held the scroll up by one end and forced me to read all the sins that I had committed in my entire life. Finally after about an hour of reading all the sinful things that I had done, it seemed as though Hell was going to open up and I was going to fall down into the horrible pit. In desperation, I reached out and took hold of the scroll and unrolling it one more turn, I read, "But the blood of Jesus Christ, God's Son, cleanses us from all sin."

The Bible clearly teaches, "If we confess our sins, he is faithful and just and will forgive us our sins" (1 John 1:9). Luther knew that, and I hope you do too.

Jacob said, "Please tell me your name." But he replied, "Why do you ask my name?" Then he blessed him there. So Jacob called the place Peniel, saying, "It is because I saw God face to face, and yet my life was spared." (Gen. 32:29–30)

During his time of struggle, Jacob faced God, confessed his weaknesses, and committed his life to Him. That's how he received a new name. His new name was Israel, which means two things: "He who struggles with God" and "Prince of God." The moment Jacob began to worship God, a new name was written down in heaven! What an incredible gift. That event anticipates the words of the apostle Paul: "Therefore, if anyone is in Christ, he is a new creation; the old has gone, the new has come!" (2 Cor. 5:17).

Praise and worship are keys to the heart of God. Pause for a moment and focus on the following praise verses:

> **Psalm 8:2**—"From the lips of children and
> infants you have ordained praise because
> of your enemies, to silence the foe and the
> avenger."
>
> **Psalm 34:1**—"I will extol the Lord at all times;
> his praise will always be on my lips."
>
> **Psalm 48:1**—"Great is the Lord, and most
> worthy of praise, in the city of our God, his
> holy mountain."
>
> **Psalm 145:21**—"My mouth will speak in praise
> of the Lord. Let every creature praise his
> holy name for ever and ever."

> Psalm 150:1–2—"Praise the LORD. Praise God
> in his sanctuary; praise him in his mighty
> heavens. Praise him for his acts of power;
> praise him for his surpassing greatness."
> James 5:13—"Is any one of you in trouble? He
> should pray. Is anyone happy? Let him sing
> songs of praise."

Not long ago, my wife and I had lunch with Peggy Benson, wife of the late Bob Benson, one of my favorite writers. As we conversed, I told Peggy how much I enjoyed her new book, *Listening for a God Who Whispers.* As we continued to talk, the conversation moved to the matters of loneliness and grief. Peggy began to share how she had built altars throughout her house. She revealed the various ways in which she practiced the presence of God through worship. Peggy told me that she was overcoming her grief and feelings of loneliness through the worship of God and a simple faith in the promises of God. She cited Ephesians 3:17 as the choice Scripture for her home: "So that Christ may dwell in your hearts through faith. And I pray that you, being rooted and established in love …" We concluded our luncheon with Peggy's poignant words: "Every day I celebrate the presence of Christ in my home, and I am not alone!"

CHANGED THROUGH TRUST

"The sun rose above him as he passed Peniel, and he was limping because of his hip" (Gen. 32:31). Have you ever wondered why God caused Jacob to walk with a limp the rest of his life? Many scholars believe that his physical disability was a reminder of his need to trust

God on a daily basis. Are you like Jacob? Do you need to change? You can, but you cannot do it alone. You must have God's help!

I was reminded of that truth when I read about Don Bennett, a Seattle businessman, who decided to climb Washington's Mount Ranier. It's a stiff climb to the peak of the 14,410-foot summit, but so many individuals have made the climb that it no longer merits getting their names in the newspaper. For Don Bennett, however, the climb was a remarkable achievement, and national papers carried the news. Why? He was the first amputee ever to reach Mount Ranier's summit. It's true that "everything is possible for him who believes" (Mark 9:23).

In the book *The Leadership Challenge*, Barry Posner tells the story of how Bennett made the climb on one leg and two crutches. Asked by reporters to share the most important lesson he learned from his celebrated climb, Bennett spoke of the team of individuals who helped him attain his dream. "You can't do it alone," he said.

> *When you're through changing, you're through.*
> —Bruce Barton

I can attest to the positive changes God has brought in my life through personal challenges. Three years ago, my wife, Linda, and I sat in a hospital room waiting for Dr. Michael Santi, her physician, to visit us. She had been diagnosed with colon cancer and was scheduled for surgery the next day.

He entered Linda's room with his usual smile, sat down on the edge of her bed, and proceeded to explain what would take place in the operating room the following morning. Frankly, we were scared to death! But when he finished explaining the surgery, recovery time, etc., he calmly took Linda by the hands and held them heavenward.

"Linda," he said, "tomorrow our hands will be in His hands." Then he prayed the most magnificent prayer: "God, I cannot do this alone," he said. "I need Your help."

This was our first indication that Dr. Santi was a believer. What a God! In the midst of our frightening experience, God gave us a Christian doctor!

As I write this, I am seated in a waiting room of that same hospital. Linda has just had her annual checkup. It has been exactly three years since she had colon cancer surgery. Dr. Santi smiles as he enters the room.

"I have good news for you. Your wife is doing great—no sign of cancer or polyps anywhere!"

I can celebrate just as Jeremiah did: "Ah, Sovereign LORD, you have made the heavens and the earth by your great power and outstretched arm. Nothing is too hard for you" (Jer. 32:17).

Yes, through the hands of a skilled surgeon, the prayers of God's people, and the encouragement of loved ones, my wife has been healed.

In retrospect, I can testify that we were changed through this event. While cancer is certainly a cruel disease, God is greater than any health problem we may encounter. You can trust Him with your troubles!

He's the Master of the mighty
He's the Captain of the conquerors
He's the Head of the heroes

He's the Leader of the legislators
He's the Overseer of the overcomers
He's the Governor of governors
He's the Prince of princes
He's the King of kings
He's the Lord of lords!
YOU CAN TRUST HIM!

—S. M. Lockridge

Throughout Linda's bout with cancer, we were encouraged to trust God through five very simple ways:

1. The prayers of God's people.
2. The presence of our family members.
3. A Christian doctor.
4. The ministry of several pastor friends, but especially Ken Southerland, who drove seven hundred miles to minister to us.
5. Cards and letters, especially the one reprinted below. It was sent to me by a cancer patient, Irene Williams, who is now in heaven where she has perfect health!

What Cancer Can't Do

Cancer is so limited ...

It cannot cripple love, it cannot shatter hope,

It cannot corrode faith, it cannot eat away peace,

It cannot destroy confidence,

It cannot kill friendship,

It cannot shut out memories,

It cannot silence courage,

It cannot invade the soul,

It cannot reduce eternal life,

It cannot quench the spirit,

It cannot lessen the power of the resurrection.

Though the physical body may be destroyed by disease, the spirit can remain triumphant. If disease has invaded your body, refuse to let it touch your spirit. Your body can be severely afflicted, and you may have a struggle. But if you keep trusting God's love, your spirit will remain strong.

Why must I bear this pain? I cannot tell: I only know my
Lord does all things well. And so trust in God, my all in
all, for He will bring me through, what'er befall.

Our greatest enemy is not disease, but despair.
                                        —Source Unknown

As a result of the cancer crisis in our home, I have reached the
conclusion that all good things come from God's hand. Our home,
children, food, flowers, music, sunsets, rain, snow, and—most of
all—*life* reflect His unconditional love.

*Ask and it will be given to you; seek and you will find; knock
and the door will be opened to you. (Matt. 7:7)*

Please pray this simple prayer with me now:

Lord, as I begin this new day, I am resolved to break free
of Satan's chains and *change*. I am Your expectant child.
Holy Spirit, work in my life to change me for the better.
In Jesus' name, amen!

CHAPTER 13

Never Check Your Oil While Parked on a Hill

It was a beautiful, sunny day. There was not a cloud in the sky! The pilot, Tom Hawk, a World Relief Missions pilot, was busy showing David Vaughn and me the countryside. Flying from Ohio to Virginia was an exhilarating experience! The mountains were breathtaking as we flew over my beloved West Virginia, and as we approached the Virginia border, it appeared that I would be right on schedule for my speaking engagement in Richmond.

In the distance, we could see heavy clouds, and rain began to descend on our Cherokee Piper. Nervously, our pilot called the Richmond tower. That's when we discovered that he wasn't instrument rated.

For the next hour, Tom spoke with the air controller, who guided us skillfully down through the clouds and to the ground. The moments in the sky were so tense that no one mentioned the potential danger we were facing.

When we got out of the plane, my friend David, as pale as a ghost, knelt down and kissed the pavement! "Now I know why the pope kisses the ground every time he gets out of a plane!" he said. He had echoed my sentiments exactly. I had been scared to death! What tremendous relief to be safe on the ground again!

Don't despair. Even the sun has a sinking spell every
night, but it rises again in the morning!

Fear can have a great impact on a person, but it can be overcome. While he was assistant secretary of the navy, Franklin Roosevelt was stricken with polio. Through exercise and therapy, he was able to regain the use of his hands and was able to shuffle his feet and take a few steps with the use of a brace. Friends encouraged him to back off and take life easy. Although he could have done that because he was a wealthy man, he was determined to become a public servant. Soon he became governor of New York. Eleven years later, he became the thirty-second president of the United Sates.

Roosevelt was also a man who admittedly had a fear of fire. He was especially afraid that he would one day be in his office in his wheelchair and not be able to get out of the building if it caught fire. On the day of his inauguration as president, America was in the midst of a great depression, and one out of every four men in America was unemployed. Roosevelt shuffled to the lectern, and said boldly, "The only thing we have to fear is fear itself." He spoke from experience, having conquered many of his own fears.

Recently I had the privilege of eating dinner with Rick Stanley, the stepbrother of Elvis Presley, and Dr. Nelson Price, pastor for the past thirty years of the great First Baptist Church of Rowell, Georgia. The conversation moved from stories by Rick Stanley about his brother, Elvis, to Civil War stories told by Dr. Price.

As Dr. Price recounted a Stone Mountain Civil War shutdown, he began to talk about the anxieties that plagued the Confederate soldiers. I was captivated by a statement that he made about fear. He said, "Fear robs the mind of reason and the ability to act!"

Without doubt, we live in a world of fear. According to psychiatrist James Reich,

- 3 percent of the population of the United State experience panic
- 6 percent agoraphobia
- 3 percent generalized anxiety
- More than 2 percent simple phobias (fear of a specific situation, object, creature, activity, or experience)
- Nearly 2 percent social phobias (dread of situations in which they may be observed by others in such acts as eating, speaking, writing, vomiting, or urinating).

Research by the National Institute of Mental Health shows that phobias and related anxiety disorders are the *most common psychological problems* in America. More than 13 million people are affected.[52]

One of the saddest things is that children are subject to terrible fears too. Donald Medeiros stated in his book *Children Under Stress* that "more than six out of ten children in our land between the ages of seven and eleven report that they are afraid someone will break into their house and hurt them." After interviewing 2,200 children, Medeiros concluded in his book, "Twenty-five percent of the children said that they were afraid they might be hurt when they left their house. And in all types of neighborhoods more than 50 percent of the children said they think their neighborhood is not a very good place to grow up."[53]

People's fears run the gamut. In a recent survey, *Psychology Today* polled its readers to find out what they were afraid of. More than one thousand responded. Elizabeth Stark wrote, "Respondents chose death of a loved one overwhelmingly as their greatest fear. This was followed by serious illness. Financial worries and nuclear war tied for third."[54]

And Denis Waitley, in his book *Seeds of Greatness*, told of a University of Michigan study done on fear in relationship to reality. The study indicated that 60 percent of our fears are totally unwarranted; that is, the things we fear never come to pass. Twenty percent of our fears have already become past activities. That is, they are completely out of our control. Ten percent of our fears are so petty they don't make any difference at all. Of the remaining 10 percent, only 4 or 5 percent are real and justifiable fears.[55]

Whether real or imagined, fears plague everyone—even tough professional athletes! I enjoy stories about Vince Lombardi, the famous coach of the Green Bay Packers. Forrest Gregg, a rock-hard lineman, once stated, "Even the toughest of linemen was no match against Lombardi. When he said, 'Sit down!' we didn't even bother to look for a chair!"

FEAR IS A REALITY

During the fourth watch of the night Jesus went out to them, walking on the lake. When the disciples saw him walking on the lake, they were terrified. "It's a ghost," they said, and cried out in fear. (Matt. 14:25–26)

Children in Bloomington, Illinois, were asked by their teacher, "If you could talk to President Lincoln, what would be the one question you would ask?" One child raised his hand and said, "I would ask him, 'Mr. Lincoln, were you afraid when you started first grade?'"

I can identify with that young man! As a child, I was afraid of rides at the circus. One time in particular I remember riding the Octopus, a fast-moving ride that went up and down so rapidly it took your breath away.

"Let me off this ride," I screamed. "I'm sick!" The man attending to the ride found this humorous, and despite my mother's plea to stop the ride, he cranked it up another notch. As a result, I threw up, people scurried for safety, and I did stop the ride!

In righteousness you will be established: Tyranny will be far from you; you will have nothing to fear. Terror will be far removed; it will not come near you. (Isa. 54:14)

A friend named Jim Wilcox told me the story of his twin brother, John, who is terrified of roller coasters. Despite this overwhelming fear, however, Jim convinced John to join him on one during a recent visit to the boardwalk in Santa Cruz, California. As the two-man car reached the top of the first peak, Jim noticed that John was gripping the bar so tightly his knuckles were nearly glowing white. When Jim turned to tease John about his phobic behavior, he saw John's lips moving, but it wasn't until they started down that first drop at fifty miles per hour that his whisper reached a crescendo: "I hate you! I hate you! I hate you!"—a refrain he was to continue throughout his entire ordeal.

There have been many times of great fear in my life. One came when my father was killed in a construction accident. For some time after that, I feared everything—teachers, changing classes, sleeping alone at night, and the neighborhood bully!

As I moved into my teen years, another fear plagued me: working on my 1959 Rambler. I have never been mechanical (I can barely make toast), but I had received instructions from my stepfather to check my oil regularly. So I did. The first time I checked the oil in my Rambler, it was parked on the side of hill and the dipstick showed *empty!* Boy, was I scared! I hurried to the nearest filling station to pour in a quart of 10W-40. Before I could complete the task, a helpful attendant looked and found that my dipstick now registered full. I thought it was a miracle! I later found out that you should never check your oil while parked on a hill.

> *Don't be afraid of the day you have never seen.*
> —English Proverb

One evening a pastor in the Los Angeles area was upstairs at home cleaning a rare gun from his collection. Though he didn't know it, one of his deacons had stopped by and was downstairs visiting with his wife when the gun accidentally discharged. The accident had the potential to be disastrous, but luckily, the bullet didn't hit anyone. Some good did come out of the incident, however. From that day forward the pastor's board consisted of six yes men.

Fear goes back a long way in human history, all the way back to Adam when he said, "I heard you in the garden, and I was afraid" (Gen. 3:10). And many of our fears are genuine. Harold Kushner, in his book *When All You've Ever Wanted Isn't Enough,* clarified the difference between fear and awe.

> Fear is a negative emotion. It is constructing. It makes us either want to run away from what we are afraid of, or destroy it. It makes us feel angry and resentful, angry at the person or thing that frightens us, and angry at our own weakness which leaves us vulnerable. To obey God out of fear is to serve Him sullenly and with only part of ourselves.

> But awe is a positive feeling, an expansive feeling. Where fear makes us want to run away, awe makes us draw closer even as we hesitate to get too close. Instead of resenting our own smallness or weakness, we stand open-mouthed in appreciation of something greater than ourselves. To stand at the edge of a steep cliff and look down is to experience fear. We want to get out of that situation as quickly and safely as we can. To stand securely on a mountaintop and look around us is to feel awe. We could linger there forever.[56]

In the case of Peter, when he saw Jesus walking on the water, he was terrified and cried out:

> *"Lord, if it's you … tell me to come to you on the water."*
> *"Come," he said.*
> *Then Peter got down out of the boat, walked on the water and came toward Jesus. But when he saw the wind, he was afraid*

and, beginning to sink, cried out, "Lord, save me!" (Matt. 14:28–30)

Peter looked to Christ and began walking once again on the water. The key to victory over your fears is to keep your focus on God. Keep your eyes on Him, and you will stay on top of your fears.

The Bible repeats the command "Fear not!" hundreds of times.

FEAR IS RELATED TO DOUBT

Immediately Jesus reached out his hand and caught him. "You of little faith," he said, "why did you doubt?" (Matt. 14:31)

Both faith and fear may sail into your harbor, but allow only faith to drop anchor.

When Peter lost his focus, he began to doubt. My guess is that Peter didn't know how to swim! He began to sink, and, scared to death, he cried out, "Lord, save me!"

The word *fear* comes from the Old English *faer*, meaning sudden danger. It refers to fright where fright is justified. It refers to danger that is concrete, real, and knowable. In such cases, fear is appropriate and sometimes useful to help us escape harm.

Of course, all fears are not justified. In an interview Steve Allen once had with a doctor, Allen's guest said to him, "The only two really instinctive fears in men are the fear of loud noises and the fear of falling. What are you afraid of, Mr. Allen?"

Without skipping a beat, Steve Allen responded, "I have a great fear of making a loud noise while falling."

We always hope
And in all things it is better
To hope than to despair.
When we return to real
Trust in
God there will
No longer be room in our
Soul for fear.
—Goethe

DELIVERANCE FROM FEAR

Even legitimate fears can be given over to God! What is your greatest fear? Psalm 34:4 says, "I sought the LORD, and he answered me; he delivered me from all my fears." Don't you think that Peter, at the very moment Jesus reached out to him, might have thought about this psalm? Perhaps he began to hum Psalm 34 and thought, "Why did I doubt Him in the first place?"

All our fret and worry is caused by calculating without God.
—Oswald Chambers

Paul reminded us in 2 Timothy 1:7 (KJV), "For God hath not given us the spirit of fear." It is not God's plan to make us fearful. But every opportunity to be fearful is an opportunity to trust God! Let me give you some steps to help you be free of fear.

1. Choose faith instead of doubt. Several years ago in Lancaster, Ohio, I heard Dr. E. Stanley Jones preach. He was a missionary statesman and a man of great faith. His words of wisdom about overcoming worry and fear were so inspiring that I wrote them in the front of my New Testament:

> I see that I am inwardly fashioned for faith and not for fear. Fear is not my native land; faith is. I am so made that worry and anxiety are sand in the machinery of life: faith is oil. I live better by faith and confidence than by fear and doubt and anxiety. In anxiety and worry, my being is gasping for breath—these are not my native air. But in faith and confidence, I breathe freely—these are my native air.

Perhaps you have heard the story of eighteen-year-old John Thompson from Hurdsfield, North Dakota. John had been working alone on the family farm. While operating a combine, his arms got caught, causing one to be amputated at the shoulder and the other at the elbow.

John freed himself from the machine and went to the farmhouse. Remaining calm, he managed to open the door with his teeth, stumble to the push-button phone in the office, and use his nose to dial a friend to ask him to call for an ambulance. He then went and sat in the bathtub and waited for the emergency medical technicians to arrive. Why the bathtub? He didn't want to get blood on his mother's carpet!

When the ambulance arrived and the technicians saw John, they were horrified! John remained cool and collected. In fact, he instructed the technicians where to find his arms and even reminded them to pack them in ice from the family freezer.

Surgeons in Minneapolis, Minnesota, were able to reattach John's arms, and he is doing extremely well.

What a courageous young man! John could have panicked in fear. He could have lain down and died alone. But he chose not to. Instead he demonstrated his faith in God by willing himself to live and making the right decisions in the most difficult circumstances. His choice to live was rewarded greatly by God. What a bright future that young man has!

> *He can give only according to His might; therefore,*
> *He always gives more than we ask for.*
> —Martin Luther

2. Turn to God's Word for strength. The following verses have strengthened me in moments when I have been tempted to be fearful.

> Psalm 34:7—"The angel of the LORD encamps around those who fear him, and he delivers them."
>
> Genesis 26:24—"Do not be afraid, for I am with you; I will bless you and will increase the number of your descendants for the sake of my servant Abraham."
>
> Psalm 23:4—"Even though I walk through the valley of the shadow of death, I will fear no evil, for you are with me; your rod and your staff, they comfort me."

Psalm 91:5—"You will not fear the terror of
night, nor the arrow that flies by day."
1 John 4:18—"There is no fear in love. But
perfect love drives out fear, because fear
has to do with punishment. The one who
fears is not made perfect in love."

It takes great courage to overcome your fears and face each day.
Art Linkletter told the story of Wendy Stoker, a nineteen-year-old
freshman at the University of Florida:

Last year she placed third, just 2 1/2 points from first, in
the Iowa girls' state diving championships. She'd worked
two hours a day for four years to get there.

Now at the University of Florida, she's working twice
as hard and has earned the number-two position
on the varsity diving team, and she's aiming for the
national finals. Wendy is carrying a full academic
load, finds time for bowling, and is an accomplished
water-skier.

But perhaps the most remarkable thing about Wendy
Stoker is her typing. She bangs out forty-five words a
minute on her typewriter—with her toes.

Oh, did I fail to mention? Wendy was born without
arms.[57]

D. L. Moody used to say, "You can travel to heaven first class or second class. Second class is, "When I am afraid, I will trust in you" (Ps. 56:3). First class, "In God I trust; I will not be afraid!" (Ps. 56:11).

3. Find peace in the prayers of others. My friend Doug Carter was aboard US Airways flight 486 from Charlotte, North Carolina, to Columbus, Ohio, when at 31,000 feet over West Virginia, one of the engines exploded and blew a hole in the side of the plane. Doug described the gaping hole as about "three feet wide and six feet high." The plane immediately went into a steep dive, and when oxygen masks began to drop, some passengers screamed while others prayed aloud.

Doug told me that he felt sure that the plane would crash into the mountains, but more importantly, he said, "I had peace that I was ready to die." Incredibly, the severely damaged plane landed safely at the Charleston, West Virginia, airport. Airline spokespersons acknowledged that it had been a miracle.

Not long after this, Doug discovered from four separate individuals that they had been burdened to pray for him at the very hour his plane was en route to Columbus, Ohio. God is never late when His children call out!

Courage is fear that has said its prayers.

4. Ask God to deliver you from your fears. One thing I admire about the apostle Peter is that even though he carried a reputation as a coward, he had the ability to come back to Christ, willing to admit his fears. When Peter stepped out of the boat and began to sink, he cried out, "Lord, save me!"

God has decreed to act in response to prayer. "Ask," He
commands us. And Satan trembles for fear we will.
—Ruth Bell Graham

I grew up watching Ohio State football. I loved to go to the big horseshoe-shaped stadium and watch the Buckeyes play football. Woody Hayes, the dynamic, excitable, and often controversial football coach, one day spoke at my Northland High School assembly. Coach Hayes concluded his speech by describing his first day as head coach of the Big Ten powerhouse.

> The first time I stood in the middle of the Ohio stadium with its 86,000 seats staring down at me, I was shook up. I stood there holding my son's hand and I thought of the fans and how angry they can get if you lose. Then I thought of all the people who were depending on me to develop a winning team. For a moment I felt fearful. My young son must have sensed my fear for he gripped my hand and said, "Dad, look at the field, it's the same as all the others."

Amazing, isn't it? A child calmed his father's fears.

If it's any encouragement to you, Jesus had fears too. Look what He had to say about His fears in Matthew 26:36–43:

> *Then Jesus went with his disciples to a place called Gethsemane,*
> *and he said to them, "Sit here while I go over there and pray."*
> *He took Peter and the two sons of Zebedee along with him, and*

*he began to be sorrowful and troubled. Then he said to them,
"My soul is overwhelmed with sorrow to the point of death.
Stay here and keep watch with me." Going a little farther, he
fell with his face to the ground and prayed, "My Father, if it
is possible, may this cup be taken from me. Yet not as I will,
but as you will." Then he returned to his disciples and found
them sleeping. "Could you men not keep watch with me for one
hour?" he asked Peter. "Watch and pray so that you will not fall
into temptation. The spirit is willing, but the body is weak."
He went away a second time and prayed, "My Father, if it is
not possible for this cup to be taken away unless I drink it, may
your will be done." When he came back, he again found them
sleeping, because their eyes were heavy.*

God already knows your fears. Ask Him to extend a calming
hand to you right now. He will deliver you from your fears!

Hope is brightest when it dawns from fears.

I once heard a joke about three guys who died at the same time
and ended up in front of Saint Peter at the Pearly Gates. Saint Peter
said to the first guy, "Why should I let you in?"

The guy answered, "I was a doctor and I helped many people
get well."

Saint Peter said, "Okay, you may come in."

Saint Peter asked the second guy, "Why should I let you in?"

The guy answered, "I was a lawyer and defended many innocent
people."

Saint Peter said, "Okay, you may come in."

Saint Peter than said to the last guy, "And why should I let you in?"

The guy answered, "Well, I was a managed health care professional and I helped to keep health care costs down."

Saint Peter thought about it for a moment, then said, "Okay, you may come in, but you can stay only three days."

Fortunately, God doesn't really run heaven that way. You can depend on Him for eternity.

Try God

When troubles are deep and your world is dark,
don't give up hope, "TRY GOD" ...
When life turns sour and you've lost your way,
don't give up hope, "TRY GOD" ...
When fears stack up and you're sure no one cares,
don't give up hope, "TRY GOD" ...
When temptation comes knocking and you struggle with it so,
don't give up hope, "TRY GOD" ...

—Source Unknown

CHAPTER 14

When Nothing's Happening, Something's Happening

University of Illinois football coach Bob Zuppke was famous for his motivational halftime speeches. He really knew how to fire up his teams!

One Saturday afternoon, Zuppke's team was losing and lethargic. Coach Zuppke gave a "win one for the Gipper" kind of speech. And the troops responded excitedly. Dramatically, the coach pointed to the door at the end of the locker room and said, "Now go out there and win this game!"

Emotionally charged, the players jumped up and ran to the door. The first player blasted through the door as several others followed. But there was one problem: It was the wrong door. One by one, they all fell into the swimming pool!

Life is a lot like that! We find a door and charge through it, only to discover it's the wrong door. At other times, we think nothing's happening in our lives. But that's when we should *really* pay attention to what God is doing.

The phrase "When nothing's happening, something's happening!" took on great significance to me on an almost daily basis in my home mission church. I have often confided to friends that I enjoyed this faith-building experience more than any other phase of my ministry. It constantly required complete and utter dependence on God in the matter of church finances. In other words, we were always *broke!*

On one occasion, I took a step of faith and purchased on credit twenty-two used church pews at a cost of two thousand dollars. That was a wonderful price considering new pews would have cost us approximately eight thousand dollars. There was only one problem— I had no idea on earth how were going to pay for the pews. After all, our church offerings averaged only one hundred twenty dollars per week. What I didn't know was that God was at work behind the scenes.

I spent a very restless night walking the halls, crying, praying, and wondering why I had just spent two thousand dollars for those pews!

The very next morning, I stopped for my usual cup of coffee at Shoney's and then drove to the post office. There was only one envelope in the mailbox, and it had a window. (Usually, this meant it was a bill!) I got into the car, tossed the letter aside, and drove to my office. (I hate to open bills!) Later in the morning, I decided to open the letter. I was immediately stunned!

It was a letter from the Oldham Little Church Foundation. Two years prior to this faith venture, I had written the Oldham Little Church Foundation requesting financial help with the construction of our church sanctuary. They responded quickly to my letter turning us down. I accepted this disappointment and forgot about the whole situation. Now I was holding a letter from them in my hands:

Dear Pastor Toler,

Greetings! I am writing to inform you of the decision of Oldham Little Church Foundation board to assist you in your building program. While the enclosed check is small, we trust that it will help you purchase some pulpit furniture.

Enclosed is a check for $2,000.

As I have reflected on this incident, I am reminded that God's timing is always perfect. He knows what we need and when we need it. Personally, I have on occasion wished that He would work with my time schedule. But this I know: God is never late, and He never fails! Never!

> *Yesterday is history*
> *Tomorrow is mystery*
> *Today is a gift*
> *That's way it's called the present!*

Life certainly has its ups and downs. I once read the story of an Italian peasant man who encountered a monk from the monastery that was located on a mountain near his home village.

"Father," he said to the monk, "I've always wanted to ask you something. What do you men of God do up on that huge hill?" The man continued, "Are you closer to God up on that mountain? Tell me about the life of holiness you live up there."

The wise monk was silent for a moment, stroked his beard, and then said, "What do we men of God do up there on the holy mountain? I'll tell you what we do. We fall down, we get up. We fall down, we get up. We fall down, we get up. Quite humbling, don't you think, for holy men?"

Falling down is quite a humbling experience, yet it is very much a part of all of our lives. It certainly is essential to our spiritual development.

Learning to get along with others also has its ups and downs. Mother Teresa, speaking at the National Prayer Breakfast in Washington, D.C. in 1993, said:

> It is not enough for us to say, "I love God," but I also have to love my neighbor. St. John says that you are a liar if you say you love God, and you don't love your neighbor. How can you love God whom you do not see, if you do not love your neighbor whom you see, whom you touch, with whom you live? And so it is very important for us to realize that love, to be true, has to hurt. I must be willing to give whatever it takes not to harm other people and, in fact, to do good to them. This requires that I be willing to give until it hurts. Otherwise, there is no true love in me, and I bring injustice, not peace, to those around me.

At the heart of genuine love is forgiveness. Recently I read an article outlining the difference between theological forgiveness and psychological forgiveness. The writer suggested that theological forgiveness was the ideal, because it speaks to us about the way God loves us, forgives us, and forgets our sins. Psychological forgiveness, on the other hand, focuses on the need to forgive but also acknowledges the difficulty of forgetting.

I love to tell the story of little Johnnie, who was sitting on his front porch enjoying his candy bar when a so-called friend came by and took it from him. Johnnie ran down the street, tackled his friend, and sat down on his chest. Looking into his friend's chocolate-covered face, he said, "I could forgive you for stealing and eating my candy bar, but it would be easier to forget it if you would wipe the chocolate off your face."

We all so desperately want the forgiveness of others, and we all so desperately need God's forgiveness. Both can be achieved through a clear understanding of the following verse from the book of Ephesians: "Be kind and compassionate to one another, forgiving each other, just as in Christ God forgave you" (4:32).

You cannot shake hands with a clenched fist.

—Golda Meir

WHAT IS FORGIVENESS?

Romans 4:7–8 says, "Blessed are they whose transgressions are forgiven, whose sins are covered. Blessed is the man whose sin the Lord will never count against him."

Forgiveness from sin is an awesome thing. In his book *Will Daylight Come?* Richard Hoefler included an insightful illustration of how sin enslaves and forgiveness frees.

A little boy visiting his grandparents was given his first slingshot. Johnny practiced in the woods, but he could never hit his target. As he came back to Grandma's backyard, he spied her pet duck. On an impulse, he took aim and let it fly. The stone hit, and the duck fell dead. Johnny panicked. Desperately he hid the dead duck in the woodpile, only to look up and see his sister watching. Sally had seen it all, but she said nothing.

After lunch that day, Grandma said, "Sally, let's wash the dishes."

But Sally smiled and said, "Johnny told me he wanted to help in the kitchen today. Didn't you, Johnny?" And she whispered to him, "Remember the duck!" Johnny did the dishes.

Later Grandpa asked if the children wanted to go fishing. Grandma said, "I'm sorry, but I need Sally to help me make supper."

Sally grinned and said, "That's all taken care of. Johnny wants to do it." Again she whispered, "Remember the duck." Johnny peeled potatoes while Sally went fishing.

After several days of doing both his chores and Sally's, Johnny could stand it no longer. He confessed to his grandma that he'd killed the duck. "I know, Johnny," she said, giving him a hug. "I was standing at the window and saw the whole thing. Because I love you, I forgave you. I wondered how long you would let Sally make a slave of you."

Jesus Christ knows the things you've done wrong, but He did not come to rub them in. He came to rub them out.[58]

—Rick Warren

Blessed is he whose transgressions are forgiven, whose sins are covered. (Ps. 32:1)

FORGIVENESS MODELS THE LIFE AND EXAMPLE OF CHRIST

"And when you stand praying, if you hold anything against anyone, forgive him, so that your Father in heaven may forgive you your sins" (Mark 11:25). The true model of forgiveness is found in the life and example of Jesus.

Some years ago, while speaking at Houghton College, I had the privilege of meeting Dr. S. I. McMillen, author of *None of These Diseases*. Talking with Dr. McMillen was a stimulating experience. I shared with him that I had often quoted from his book and that perhaps his most challenging words to me centered on the matter of forgiveness, for he had once said, "The moment I start hating a man, I become his slave. He controls my thoughts. I cannot escape his grip on my mind. Hatred is a boomerang. It will return and find us instead of the intended target."

Unforgiveness does a great deal more damage to the vessel in which it is stored than the object on which it is poured.
—S. I. McMillen

Neil Anderson once said, "We must forgive in the same way we have been forgiven. In His mercy, God has given us what we need, not what we deserve." "But if you do not forgive men their sins, your Father will not forgive your sins" (Matt. 6:15).

Forgiveness is hard for us because it goes against our sense of fairness. To forgive is a conscious decision of the will. Since God commands us to do it, we know that it is possible. We need to realize that forgiveness is not just for the sake of the offender. It is also for us so we can be free.

The high cost of forgiveness comes because it involves being willing to live with the consequences of someone else's sin. Genuine forgiveness is always substitutional, just as Jesus took upon Himself the penalty of our sin. That, in fact, is our motive for forgiving: He forgave us.[59]

If your enemy is hungry, give him food to eat; if he is thirsty, give him water to drink. (Prov. 25:21)

Forgiveness is a command of Christ; therefore, every believer is obligated to endeavor to practice forgiveness. Perhaps Dr. Francis Schaffer said it best: "If I am not willing to practice forgiveness, then the world has a right to question whether Christianity is true."

I never knew a night so black
Light failed to follow on its track.
I never knew a storm so gray
It failed to have its clearing day.
I never knew such a black despair
That there was not a rift somewhere.
I never knew an hour so drear
Love could not fill it of cheer!
—John Kendrick Bangs

STAGES OF FORGIVENESS

Forgiveness is not an occasional act; it is a permanent attitude.
—Martin Luther King Jr.

Lewis Smedes, preaching at Suncoast Community Church, stated that there are four stages to forgiveness:

> **Hurt:** You feel betrayed and a victim of pain you didn't deserve.
>
> **Hate:** You want revenge from the offender for the wrong he or she did to you.
>
> **Healing:** You start to see the offender as a weak person who may use cruelty to cope with inadequacies.
>
> **Forgiveness:** You begin to have positive thoughts; at first, perhaps, you only wish the person would reform, but later you may want to consider a reconciliation.

Unless we are willing to forgive, we destroy the bridge whereby we receive and perceive God's forgiveness of us.
—Dr. David Seamands

Not long ago, my golfing friend Huston Hall brought me a tape of Adolph Coors's personal testimony. Coors grew up in the Colorado mountains, where his father built the Coors Brewing Company into a family fortune. Adolph related the story of the day his father had started driving to the brewery from their snowy mountain home when he pulled over to the side of the road to help a stranded motorist. Unwittingly, Coors had walked into a deadly trap. The supposed stranded traveler was, in fact, a murderous kidnapper. He killed Adolph's father and attempted to extort money from the family through a ransom note, but his plot was discovered and he eventually went to prison.

Adolph confessed that this childhood event caused so much bitterness and hatred in him that it tainted his adult life. Coors testified that as his marriage, career, and family crumbled around him, he sought forgiveness through the shed blood of Jesus Christ. Coors became a Christian and began to put Ephesians 4 into practice. Ultimately, Adolph Coors went to the prison cell that held his father's murderer and forgave him. What relief he experienced through this difficult experience!

> *The weak can never forgive. Forgiveness is the attribute of the strong.*
> —Mohandas K. Gandhi

While forgiveness brings tremendous relief, unforgiveness wreaks havoc in a person's life. While attending the National Association of Religious Broadcasters convention, I heard Senator Mark Hatfield recount the following story:

> James Garfield was a lay preacher and principal of his denominational college. They say he was ambidextrous and could simultaneously write Greek with one hand and Latin with the other.

In 1880, he was elected president of the United States, but after only six months in office, he was shot in the back with a revolver. He never lost consciousness. At the hospital, the doctor probed the wound with his little finger to seek the bullet. He couldn't find it, so he tried a silver-tipped probe. Still he couldn't locate the bullet.

They took Garfield back to Washington, D.C. Despite the summer heat, they tried to keep him comfortable. He was growing very weak. Teams of doctors tried to locate the bullet, probing the wound over and over. In desperation they asked Alexander Graham Bell, who was working on a little device called the telephone, to see if he could locate the metal inside the president's body. He came, he sought, and he too failed.

The president hung on through July, through August, but in September he finally died—not from the wound, but from infection. The repeated probing, which the physicians thought would help the man, eventually killed him.[60]

So it is with people who refuse to forgive and who harbor hateful feelings. Eventually, these feelings kill the human spirit.

One of my favorite *Peanuts* cartoon strips depicts Lucy chasing Charlie Brown around and around the house. "I'll get you, Charlie Brown, I'll get you!" Suddenly, Charlie Brown stops. Lucy comes to a screeching stop.

Charlie Brown says, "If we, who are children, cannot forgive one another, how can we expect our parents, who are adults, to forgive one another, and in turn, how can the world ..." At this point, Lucy punches Charlie Brown in the nose and knocks him down. Turning to a friend who had just come up, Lucy explains: "I had to hit him, he was beginning to make sense."[61]

Love is the medicine for the sickness of the world.

Forgiving Others Brings Peace

Forgiveness can turn the hardest heart soft again. Noted counselor and author Dr. J. Allan Peterson told the story of a woman who came to his office full of hatred for her husband. She told Dr. Peterson, "Before I divorce him, I want to hurt him as much as he has hurt me!"

Dr. Peterson encouraged the woman to return home and try to demonstrate love and forgiveness for thirty days. Additionally, he told her that if after thirty days of effort she still disliked him, she could consider a separation.

The woman went home and made an effort to praise her husband instead of picking at him. She decided to be helpful instead of difficult. And she began daily to express her love for him instead of hatred.

When she returned to Dr. Peterson's office after thirty days, the woman was beaming. Full of joy and enthusiasm, she said, "I don't want a divorce. I love this man!" She confessed that their relationship was healed through love, listening, giving, and forgiving.

It seems God is limited by our prayer life—that He can do
nothing for humanity unless someone asks Him.
—John Wesley

I've experienced the great healing joy of forgiving personally. Several years ago, I attended a service where my friend Dr. H. B. London Jr., later assistant to the president of Focus on the Family, was preaching. As we entered the sanctuary, each attendee received a brown paper lunch bag that was labeled "God Bag." In addition, white strips of paper were distributed to each person. As Dr. London concluded his powerful message, he asked each person in attendance to write down his or her hurts, problems, and needs and put them in the God Bag. I joined with others in making my list.

One hurt was especially painful to write down. A person whom I had employed and had trusted as a friend had betrayed me. It appeared that the lie that had been told about me would never be corrected. Because it raised questions about my integrity, I was especially hurt and upset. Day after day, I had thought about the incident, often weeping bitterly in prayer, asking God to deal with my offender.

Finally, after allowing each of us time to finish writing, Dr. London instructed each person to prayerfully commit each concern to the Lord and put them into the bag. And he told us to remove the strips of paper only as our prayers were answered.

With a sense of relief and childlike faith, I placed my concerns into the God Bag. I felt better immediately! (Yes, even about my offender.)

Daily I began praying the Lord's Prayer. In that prayer, Jesus taught us to pray, "Forgive us our debts, as we also have forgiven our debtors" (Matt. 6:12). I chose not to curse or rehearse my hurts. I cupped my hands before the Lord and symbolically gave them over to Him. I then raised my hands in prayer (both hands—pretty good for a Nazarene!) and claimed victory over my hurts!

Time passed and with each answer to prayer, I removed a strip of paper and gave thanks to God. Five years passed, and all but one strip of paper had been removed. You guessed it—there had been no contact from my offender. Then, one Saturday evening as I sat putting the finishing touches on my Sunday morning message titled "What Is Forgiveness?" the phone rang. It was the person who had attacked my credibility.

The tearful voice said, "It's been years since I've talked to you. Will you forgive me for lying about you? Christ has forgiven me, and now I need to know—Stan, will you forgive me?" Without hesitation, I said, "You have my forgiveness!"

What peace flooded my soul as I went to my office and took out the last strip of paper from the God Bag! God is never late in matters of forgiveness. He knows the very moment that our souls need relief!

It's one thing to understand forgiveness. It's another to experience the power of it personally. I want to recommend several action steps to assist you in finding healing for your hurts.

ACTION STEPS TO FORGIVENESS

Step 1: List the names of people who have offended you.

Get rid of all bitterness, rage and anger, brawling and slander, along with every form of malice. Be kind and compassionate to one another, forgiving each other, just as in Christ God forgave you. (Eph. 4:31–32)

Step 2: Place their names in a God Bag.

But I tell you: Love your enemies and pray for those who persecute you. (Matt. 5:44)

Step 3: Pray daily for each offender by name.

Perhaps a plan developed by Robert Muller will assist you in crystallizing a prayer strategy. Muller suggested the following:

> Sunday—forgive yourself
>
> Monday—forgive your family
>
> Tuesday—forgive your friends and associates
>
> Wednesday—forgive across economic lines
> within your own nation
>
> Thursday—forgive across cultural lines within
> your own nation
>
> Friday—forgive across political lines within your
> own nation
>
> Saturday—forgive other nations

But I tell you, Do not resist an evil person. If someone strikes you on the right cheek, turn to him the other also. (Matt. 5:39)

Step 4: Ask God to forgive you for the spirit of unforgiveness.

"Take heart ... your sins are forgiven" (Matt. 9:2). Releasing a spirit of unforgiveness can bring about a transformation in your life. Legend tells us that the beautiful Helen of Troy, over whom many battles were fought, was lost after one of the battles. When the army returned to Greece, Helen was not on any of the ships. Menelaus went to try to find her, at great personal peril. He finally found her in one of the seaport villages. She had been suffering from amnesia. Forgetting who she was, she had stooped to the lowest possible level and was living as a prostitute.

Menelaus found her living in rags, dirt, shame, and dishonor. He looked at her and called, "Helen." Her head turned. "You are Helen of Troy!" he said. And with those words, her back straightened and the royal look came back. Similarly, God can bring about change in you.

A Short Course in Human Relations

The six most important words: "I admit I made a mistake,"
The five most important words: "You did a good job."
The four most important words: "What is your opinion?"
The three most important words: "If you please."
The two most important words: "Thank you."
The one most important word: "We."
The least important word: "I."
—Source Unknown

Step 5: Make a commitment "to forgive as Christ has forgiven you...."

Step 6: Take a step toward repairing a fractured relationship.

*Do not judge, and you will not be judged. Do not condemn,
and you will not be condemned. Forgive, and you will be
forgiven. (Luke 6:37)*

No relationship is beyond repair. No person is beyond forgiveness.
A *20/20* news segment told the story of Katherine Ann Power, who
confessed her role in a 1970 bank robbery in which Officer Walter
Schroeder was killed. What a frightening tale of teen rebellion she
unfolded.

On September 17, 1993, the *New York Times* carried an interview story with the nephew of Officer Schroeder. A genuine attitude
of forgiveness and reconciliation was evident in the words of Office
Schroeder's nephew.

"I was very angry back then," he said. "If you had asked me then,
I would have said, 'Put her up against the wall and shoot her. I would
have loved to have taken her to my aunt's house to show her what she
did to those nine children.'"

But as the interview continued, Mr. Schroeder said, "I find
myself forgiving Ms. Power now. For forty-nine years, I was taught to
forgive—by my church, by my father. It gets embedded in you more
and more as you get older. There's no use in hating people."

*General Oglethorpe once said to John Wesley, "I never forgive and I never
forget." To which Wesley responded, "Then, Sir, I hope you never sin."*

CHAPTER 15

Okay, God, If You're Listening, Why Aren't You Answering?

There is a story about two Catholic nuns who were out delivering medical supplies to a nursing home when their car ran out of gas. They searched in the trunk of the car for a gas can, but could find only a bedpan. The sisters walked a half mile to a gas station and filled the bedpan with gas.

Upon returning to their car, they carefully balanced the bedpan and started to pour the gas into the tank. About that time a man driving a pickup truck approached, and as he saw what was going on, he came to a complete stop. Marveling at what he *thought* he was seeing, he stuck his head out of the truck window and said, "Sisters, I'm not Catholic, but I'll tell you what. I sure do admire your faith!"

The Word of God clearly promises that God hears and answers our prayers, although at times it appears that He is not listening. Why is it that some of our prayers seem to get through to God and others seem to fall on deaf ears?

There are no easy answers, said Dr. James Dobson in *When God Doesn't Make Sense*. In 1987, four of Dr. Dobson's best friends were killed in a plane crash on their way home from a Focus on the Family retreat in Montana. Why did they die, leaving wives and children to carry on alone?

Dobson said that life is filled with many examples of unexplainable pain and suffering brought upon godly people. Are these events evidence of God's wrath or something else? How do we explain these tragedies and others that strike both Christian and non-Christian alike? The Lord has not made it clear in the Bible why these things happen. What His Word does tell us is that we lack the capacity to understand God's infinite mind or the way He chooses to intervene in our lives.

"It is an incorrect view of Scripture to say that we will always comprehend what God is doing and how our suffering and disappointment fit into His plan," Dobson said. It is like *confusion* that shreds one's faith.

"Expectations," Dobson wrote, "set us up for disillusionment. There's no greater distress than to build one's entire life around certain theological beliefs and then have those beliefs collapse when tragedy strikes."

Dr. Dobson gave the following four principles he has learned over the years about God working in our lives:

1. God is present and involved in our lives, even when He seems deaf or absent.
2. God's timing is perfect, even when He appears catastrophically late.
3. For reasons that are impossible to explain, we human beings are incredibly precious to God.

4. Our arms are too short to box with God. Don't
even try.[62]

Dobson then told hurting readers to expect confusing circumstances and to embrace them as opportunities for faith to grow. After I read his book, my mind drifted back twelve years to the events surrounding the birth of our youngest son, Adam.

I had just closed my eyes for a brief afternoon nap. The conference in Dayton, Ohio, where I was speaking seemed to have drained all the energy out of me. That's when the phone rang, disturbing my sleep. The caller asked me to hurry to the Fayette County Hospital where my wife, Linda, had gone into labor. Moments after I arrived, Adam James Toler was born prematurely into the world, weighing a whopping eight pounds and ten ounces!

As I laid my head on the pillow just after midnight, I began to focus on the Sunday morning service at Heritage Memorial Church. I was tired but anxious to tell the congregation about the birth of our second son.

At 4:00 a.m., the phone rang. It was the doctor.

"Come to the hospital quickly; Adam is having some difficulty," he said. I hustled to get dressed and rushed to the hospital in record time!

As I arrived, I noticed that the infant care mobile unit from Children's Hospital was parked at the emergency entrance of the Fayette County Hospital. Nurses met me at the door to explain that doctors had performed emergency surgery, and it would be necessary to take Adam to the Columbus Children's Hospital. After meeting with Dr. Chang, we agreed that Adam needed a moment to bond with his mother before leaving the hospital. Because of an infection that Adam had developed and his difficulty breathing, the two had not yet experienced a mother-son moment.

As the nurse lifted Adam from his incubator and presented him to his mother for the first time, hot tears poured from my eyes. Watching Linda hold Adam for that first moment and realizing that he might not live for another hour was overwhelming. Linda kissed Adam good-bye and watched intently as they rolled his incubator from the room. As I hugged Linda, our tears mingled with the haunting thought that our son might not live through the day.

"Linda," I said through tears, "who pastors the pastor? All these years of ministry, I have stood by and encouraged others. I've prayed prayers of comfort for many families, and here we are alone!"

Linda pulled me down close then prayed a beautiful prayer of thanks for Adam and boldly asked God for a miracle.

> *Sometimes God calms the raging storm. Sometimes*
> *He lets the storm rage and calms His child.*[63]
> —Barbara Johnson

Driving to Children's Hospital in Columbus, Ohio, gave me time for thought and prayer. I pulled myself together, followed the medical team to the Infant Care Unit on the second floor, and braced myself for the worst.

To my surprise, there were more than thirty premature infants in that unit at Children's Hospital. Some of the babies weighed less than two pounds, and were smaller than my hand. Adam looked like a "giant among mortals." But he was a sick baby, with a collapsed lung and a condition termed "serious."

Days and hours passed by. To my surprise, my church family was gracious and caring. They watched over Linda in the Fayette County Hospital, and they made arrangements for my in-laws, James and Nadine Carter, to come to Ohio from South Georgia to watch over our four-year-old, Seth. They conducted daily prayer vigils at church and visited me regularly at the hospital. During all of their caregiving, I began to realize the importance of lay ministry. And I discovered that laypersons can pastor the pastor!

While I was at Children's Hospital, I spent a lot of time with Adam. He was strapped down with tubes running everywhere, always flat on his back. He rarely moved or made a sound. My job at the hospital was to be near him and to constantly touch him. It was the nurses' view that a parent's touch was very important to the recovery of the child. I couldn't agree more. The healing from that contact was going both directions.

On the third day, after taking a short lunch break, I returned to the Infant Care Unit only to encounter nurses who explained that Adam had taken a turn for the worse.

"He may not live through the day," they said. Because they were performing emergency procedures, I was not allowed in the room. Hurriedly, I went to a phone and began to call friends from California to Virginia, asking them to pray for Adam. Hundreds gathered at Heritage Memorial Church for prayer. Heaven was being bombarded for Adam James!

Two hours passed, and a nurse came to get me. A weak feeling went through my inner being. I was not optimistic. As I approached

Adam, I noticed that he was face down on the bed, no diaper, his rear end sticking up in the air—and there was movement! I asked the nurse, "What does this mean?"

"Pastor," she explained, "it's the 'butt' sign."

"The butt sign?" I inquired.

"Yes, sir," she explained. "When we turn them over on their tummy, it means they are going to make it! Sir, your prayers have been answered. You have a healthy son, and he'll be going home soon!"

I was in a state of shock. "God has healed my son," I cried.

What rejoicing I felt that day. How ashamed I was of my own lack of faith, and yet how thrilled I was at the faith of my brothers and sisters in Christ. They had touched God for me!

God is never late when you need a miracle!

> *Faith is the vitamin that makes all we take from the Bible digestible and makes us able to receive it and assimilate it. If we do not have faith, we cannot get anything.*
>
> —A. W. Tozer

RELEASE YOUR FAITH RIGHT NOW!

Does it seem like your prayers are not being answered? Release your faith right now and believe that God in heaven hears and answers prayer!

> *God's promise is as good as His presence.*
>
> —Andrew Murray

FAITH-BUILDING EXERCISES

"Now faith is being sure of what we hope for and certain of what we do not see. This is what the ancients were commended for" (Heb. 11:1–2). The Word of God mentions the words *faith* or *believe* 485 times. Faith occurs twenty-three times in the eleventh chapter of Hebrews alone.

As I conclude this book, please allow me to give you seven important steps to faith building. While it is true that "God has never failed me," it is also a reality that I have practiced the following faith principles.

If it is to be, it is up to God—and me!

Step 1: Study the Promises of God.

Award-winning author Philip Yancey described two kinds of faith in an article titled "When God Seems Silent." First Yancey discussed seed faith. It is the David-meeting-Goliath-*with-God-all-things-are-possible*-kind of faith. Secondly, he talked about fidelity—the "hang on at any cost" faith like that of Job.[64]

In my opinion, both faith systems work. Fred Price uses the metaphor of flying an airplane to describe faith. Scripture says that the life of victory is a matter of walking by faith, not by sight (2 Cor. 5:7). In Price's view, it's a matter of flying by the instruments—by the Word of God—when the fog is so heavy we can't see out the windows of our aircraft. It's a matter of fighting the good fight of faith—but we go into the ring already knowing who wins.[65] We must leave the realm of our senses and make our spiritual reference point the promises of God.

For a real faith-lift, review daily the promises of God. Listed below are a few promises that have helped me immensely:

- **God promises to hear my prayers.** "Before they call I will answer; while they are still speaking I will hear" (Isa. 65:24).
- **God promises to reward my faithfulness.** "For the Son of Man is going to come in his Father's glory with his angels, and then he will reward each person according to what he has done" (Matt. 16:27).
- **God promises His presence in my life.** "And teaching them to obey everything I have commanded you. And surely I am with you always, to the very end of the age" (Matt. 28:20).
- **God promises to help me when I call.** "All that the Father gives me will come to me, and whoever comes to me I will never drive away" (John 6:37).
- **God promises to turn my tears into triumphs.** "And we know that in all things God works for the good of those who love him, who have been called according to his purpose" (Rom. 8:28).
- **God promises to put an end to sin and death.** "He will wipe every tear from their eyes. There will be no more death or mourning or crying or pain, for the old order of things has passed away" (Rev. 21:4).

Our faith connects us with God. Ruth Vaughn, quoting her mother, said, "You must have deep within you the consciousness that there is a God, that He loves you, and that you are in His hands."[66] This can happen only when our faith is based on God's promises.

Every promise in the Book is mine,
Every chapter, every verse, every line.
And I'm living in His love divine,
Every promise in the Book is mine.
—John Bayman

Step 2: Demonstrate Faithful Obedience to God.

John Wesley once said, "God has appointed faith to supply the defect of sense, to take us up where sense lets us down, and to help us over the gulf." If encouraged, that reassuring faith grows—from that of a servant, with *obedience* based in fear, to that of a son who obeys God out of love.

When God sees our faithful obedience in the most difficult times, He promises to see us through!

> *Remember those earlier days after you had received the light,*
> *when you stood your ground in a great contest in the face*
> *of suffering. Sometimes you were publicly exposed to insult*
> *and persecution; at other times you stood side by side with*
> *those who were so treated. You sympathized with those in*
> *prison and joyfully accepted the confiscation of your property,*
> *because you knew that you yourselves had better and lasting*
> *possessions. (Heb. 10:32–34)*

As you obey God, you often have to disregard the negative voices that come from the crowd. Rebecca Olson, in an article for *Decision* magazine, said:

The story of Noah is an example of the truth that the crowd is often wrong. Noah stood against public opinion for 120 years because his heart and mind were set on a predetermined course: one that he believed in fully. Another reason was that his outward life matched his convictions; he practiced what he preached. Noah was also assured of success because he knew the master plan.

Noah realized he was the one to influence the crowd, rather than the one who was influenced by it. He established a priority and then for 120 years, day after day, his hands built the ark while his mouth proclaimed salvation. To stand against a crowd for Jesus requires courage, action, a consistent life, obedience, and a knowledge of God's clear instructions.[67]

Step 3: Spend Time with People of Faith.

Even Jesus Christ was careful to resist the influence of unbelievers. Christians must be careful to resist the vain philosophies, values, and unbeliefs of non-Christians. We must surround ourselves with people of faith.

So do not throw away your confidence; it will be richly rewarded. You need to persevere so that when you have done the will of God, you will receive what he has promised. For in just a very little while, "He who is coming will come and will not delay. But my righteous one will live by faith. And if he shrinks back, I will not be pleased with him." But we are not of those who shrink back and are destroyed, but of those who believe and are saved. (Heb. 10:35–39)

For years now I have intentionally spent time with positive people. Don't spend your time with pessimistic people if you need a faith-lift! All they will do is breed doubt within you.

There's a story about a little girl who was afraid of storms. One night lightning flashed outside her window waking her. So she crept into her parents' bedroom and shook her mother awake, "I'm scared," she said.

"What?" asked the groggy mom.

"I'm scared, and I want to sleep with you." Somewhat more awake, the mother gave her daughter a gentle hug and tried to comfort her.

"There's nothing to be afraid of. It's just a storm. Everything is okay. Now, you go on back to your bedroom and remember that God is there with you in your bed."

The small figure stood in the dark for a long moment and then said, "Mom, how about if you go sleep in there with God, and I'll sleep in here with Daddy."

Step 4: Seek the Gift of Faith in Prayer.

At once Jesus realized that power had gone out from him. He turned around in the crowd and asked, "Who touched my clothes?"

"You see the people crowding against you," his disciples answered, "and yet you can ask, 'Who touched me?'" But Jesus kept looking around to see who had done it. (Mark 5:30–32)

The woman who reached out to touch Jesus brings us to the realization that the best way to secure a mountain-moving faith relationship with God is through your obedience to Him in the little things of life. It is "faith the size of a mustard seed" that grows through the circumstances of life and brings us to the gift of faith. Every day by faith claim this wonderful gift from God!

> *My faith looks up to Thee,*
> *Thou Lamb of Calvary, Savior divine!*
> *Now hear me while I pray;*
> *Take all my guilt away.*
> *O let me from this day be wholly Thine!"*[68]
> —Ray Palmer

Step 5: Read Biographies of Faithful Christians.

I have been reading biographies of great people since I was in grade school. People of faith stretch me mightily in my relationship with the Lord. Over the years, I have enjoyed reading biographies of Bresee, Moody, Wesley, Asbury, Mueller, and many others.

> *God is the great I am. Am is in the present tense. He is*
> *ready to do it now, so when you pray, believe that the*
> *promises of God are yea and amen in Christ Jesus.*
> —Buddy Harrison

I especially enjoyed reading about George Mueller, one of my heroes in the faith.

George Mueller of Bristol received more than $1 million for his children's orphanage over a sixty-year period. And he never asked for a penny. How did he do it? He prayed it in!

Mueller's faith became legendary. The captain of a ship on which George Mueller was sailing told the story of a trip on which there was dense fog, and the captain was on the bridge for twenty-four hours without ever leaving the helm. Mr. Mueller came to him and said, "Captain, I have come to tell you that I must be in Quebec on Saturday afternoon."

The captain replied, "It is impossible."

"Very well, then," Mr. Mueller said, "if your ship cannot take me, God will find another way. I have never broken an engagement in fifty-seven years, and I won't start now. Let's go down into the chart room and pray."

The captain looked at Mr. Mueller and thought, *What a lunatic! I've never heard of such* ... "Mr. Mueller," he said, "do you know how dense this fog is?"

"No," he said, "my eye is not on the density of the fog, but on the living God who controls every circumstance of my life!" He knelt down and prayed a simple prayer. When he finished, the captain knelt to pray, but Mr. Mueller put his hand on the captain's shoulder and said, "Since you do not believe, don't pray. God will answer, Captain. I've known my Lord for fifty-seven years. There has never been a day when I failed to get an audience with the King."

"Get up, Captain. Open the door and you will find the fog has gone!" The captain got up, opened the door, and saw that indeed the fog was gone. And on that Saturday afternoon, George Mueller kept his engagement!

*Faith is like radar that sees through the fog—the reality of
things at a distance that the human eye cannot see.*
—Corrie ten Boom

Step 6: Testify of Your Faith in Christ.

*So the man went away and began to tell in the Decapolis how
much Jesus had done for him. And all the people were amazed.
(Mark 5:20)*

Excitement about your faith in Christ is contagious. I especially
love the enthusiasm of young converts. One young teenager who
had made a decision for Christ came to me one day wanting to be
baptized. But what he said was, "Pastor, I want to get *advertised!*" I
guess if we fulfill the Great Commission by testifying of our faith in
Christ, we are helping others to be advertised.

*Therefore go and make disciples of all nations, baptizing
them in the name of the Father and of the Son and of the
Holy Spirit, and teaching them to obey everything I have
commanded you. And surely I am with you always, to the very
end of the age. (Matt. 28:19–20)*

It is important to share the miracle of salvation with your
family and friends. Remember, a relationship with Christ is fundamental to the miraculous intervention in our lives that we all
desire.

Step 7: Expect Results!

Jesus looked at them and said, "With man this is impossible,
but with God all things are possible." (Matt. 19:26)

While watching CNN recently, I was fascinated by an interview with a man who wanted to fly and inadvertently stopped air traffic near the Los Angeles Airport. This innovative man came up with the idea of flying over his community. After anchoring his lawn chair with sturdy rope, he tied helium-filled balloons to the arm rests. He packed himself a nice lunch to enjoy while flying over his neighborhood and then strapped himself into the chair with a makeshift seat belt. He also tied on a BB gun to shoot the balloons when he began his descent back to earth.

"I cut the anchor ropes loose and expected to go about one thousand feet in the air, but instead I shot up 11,000 feet into the air!" he exclaimed. This action launched him into the traffic pattern of LAX, and it took an air force helicopter to get him down!

The CNN interviewer's final question amused me greatly. "Sir, were you scared?" he asked the weary navigator.

"Yes, I was, but wonderfully so!"

What a wonderful story! Too bad his flight didn't qualify him for frequent-flier miles. I laughed about what happened to him, but his story also got me to thinking. A balloon filled with helium is lighter than air. The balloon takes on the characteristic of that which fills it.

In a similar way, believers take on the qualities of Christ when filled with the Holy Spirit. When He takes control of your life, you identify with His traits. When He swells in you, you become more buoyant and energized to rise above the circumstances of life. With Christ in us, we can reach the heights and do the exploits He desires of us.

And now I ask you, if God performed a miracle in your life, would you be scared? Let me answer for you. Yes, you would! But wonderfully so. *God has never failed me, but He's scared me to death a few times!* He will never fail you!

NOTES

1 Leslie Miller, *USA Today*, December 21, 1994.

2 King Duncan, *Parables* (Knoxville, TN: Seven Worlds, 1993).

3 James W. Moore, *Standing on the Promises or Sitting on the Premises?* (Nashville, TN: Dimensions for Living, 1995), 62.

4 Civilla D. Marti, "His Eye Is on the Sparrow," 1905, public domain.

5 Lloyd Ogilvie, *Ask Him Anything* (Nashville, TN: Word Books, 1984).

6 Walter Knight, *Knight's Master Book of New Illustrations* (Grand Rapids, MI: Eerdmans, 1956).

7 Oswald Chambers, *My Utmost for His Highest* (Grand Rapids, MI: Discovery, 1992).

8 Earl Lee, *The Cycle of Victorious Living* (Kansas City, MO: Beacon Hill, 1971).

9 *McCartney's Illustrations* (New York: Abingdon, 1955).

10 W. Phillip Keller, *Strength of Soul* (Grand Rapids, MI: Kregel, 1993), 25.

11 G. B. F. Hallock, *Five Thousand Best Modern Illustrations* (New York: Richard R. Smith, Inc., 1931).

12 Stephen Miller, ed., *What Jesus Says about Worry* (Kansas City, MO: Beacon Hill, 1994).

13 Ibid.

14 Lloyd Ogilvie, *Freedom in the Spirit* (Eugene, OR: Harvest House, 1984).

[15] Ibid.

[16] Barbara Johnson, *Mama, Get the Hammer! There's a Fly on Papa's Head!* (Nashville, TN: Thomas Nelson, 1994), 172.

[17] Louisa M. R. Stead, "'Tis So Sweet to Trust in Jesus," 1882, public domain.

[18] Max Lucado, *The Applause of Heaven* (Dallas: Word Publishing, 1990), 32–33.

[19] John Newton, "Amazing Grace," 1779, public domain.

[20] Alexandra Kropotkin, "Homemade," *Family Concern* 15.1 (January 1991).

[21] Stuart Briscoe, *Bound for Joy* (Ventura, CA: Regal Books, 1984), 95.

[22] Civilla D. Martin, "God Will Take Care of You" 1904, public domain.

[23] David A. Seamands, *Healing for Damaged Emotions* (Colorado Springs, CO: David C. Cook, 1981), 113.

[24] Ibid., 114.

[25] Ibid., 115.

[26] Ibid., 115.

[27] Bob Greene, *Hang Time: Days and Dreams with Michael Jordan* (New York: Doubleday, 1992).

[28] Charles Swindoll, *Living Beyond the Daily Grind* (Dallas: Word Publishing, 1988).

[29] Josh McDowell and Bob Hostetler, *Josh McDowell's Handbook on Counseling Youth* (Dallas: Word Publishing, 1996).

[30] H. Norman Wright, *How to Get Along with Almost Anyone* (Dallas: Word Publishing, 1989), 15–24.

[31] Paula Schwed, comp., *I've Got Tears in My Ears from Lyin' on My Back in My Bed While I Cry Over You—Country Music's Best (and Funniest) Lines* (Kansas City, MO: Andrews McMeel, 1996).

[32] A. D. Dennison Jr., *Contemporary Illustrations for Speakers and Teachers* (Grand Rapids, MI: Zondervan, 1976).

[33] Lee Iacocca and William Novak, *Iacocca* (New York: Bantam Books, 1986).

[34] George R. Walther, *Power Talking* (New York: Putnam Adult, 1991), 227.

[35] Harold Ivan Smith, *The Jabez Principle* (Kansas City, MO: Beacon Hill, 1987), 116–117.

[36] Joseph M. Scriven, "What a Friend We Have in Jesus," 1855, public domain.

[37] Jack Kuhatschek, *The Superman Syndrome* (Grand Rapids, MI: Zondervan, 1995).

[38] Augustus M. Toplady, "Rock of Ages," 1776, public domain.

[39] Steve Farrar, *Point Man* (Portland, OR: Multnomah, 1990), 56.

[40] Terry N. Toler, "I Will Live My Life for Christ," 1969.

[41] Elisabeth Elliott, *God's Guidance: A Slow and Certain Light* (Grand Rapids, MI: Revell, 1997), 26.

[42] Dennis Rainey, *Building Your Mate's Self-Esteem* (San Bernardino, CA: Here's Life, 1986), 56–57.

[43] Joyce Hollyday, "Gratitude," *Sojourners*, June 1987, 32–33.

[44] Ernest A. Fitzgerald, *God Writes with Crooked Lines* (New York: Atheneum, 1981).

[45] Daniel S. Kennedy, *The Ultimate Marketing Plan* (Holbrook, MA: Bob Adams, Inc., 2006).

[46] Judith Sills, PhD, "10 Ways to Get the Most from Your Relationships," *McCall's*, January 1994, 68.

[47] Thomas Harris, *I'm OK, You're OK* (New York: Doubleday, 1989), 91.

[48] Max De Pree, *Leadership Is an Art* (New York: Dell, 1990), 100.

[49] Shad Helmstetter, *You Can Excel in Times of Change* (New York: Pocket Books, 1992), 145–179.

[50] Rheta Grimsley Johnson, *Good Grief: The Story of Charles M. Schulz* (New York: Pharos Books, 1989).

[51] Harold Sherman, *How to Turn Failure into Success* (Englewood Cliffs, NJ: Prentice-Hall, 1982).

[52] Robert Handly and Pauline Nell, *Beyond Fear* (New York: Rawson Associates, 1987), 9.

[53] Donald C. Medeiros, Barbara Porter, and I. David Welch, *Children Under Stress,* ed. Marlys Lehmann (Englewood Cliffs, NJ: Prentice-Hall, 1983), 89.

[54] John Haggai, *Winning over Pain, Fear and Worry* (New York: Inspirational Press, 1991).

[55] Denis Waitley, *Seeds of Greatness* (Old Tappan, NJ: Revell, 1983), 76.

[56] Harold Kushner, *When All You've Ever Wanted Isn't Enough* (New York: Penguin Books, 1986), 130–31.

[57] Art Linkletter (Chicago: Nightingale-Conant Corporation, 1983), single cassette recording, quoted in Ted Engstrom, *High Performance* (San Bernardino, CA: Here's Life Publishers, 1988), 100.

[58] Rick Warren, *The Power to Change Your Life* (Wheaton, IL: Victor Books, 1990), 9.

[59] Neil Anderson, "The Bondage Breaker," *Spirit of Revival*, August 1993, 8–9.

[60] Craig Larson, ed., *Illustrations for Preaching and Teaching* (Grand Rapids, MI: Baker Books, 1993).

[61] Rheta Grimsley Johnson, *Good Grief: The Story of Charles M. Schulz* (New York: Pharos Books, 1989), 46.

[62] James Dobson, *When God Doesn't Make Sense* (Wheaton, IL: Tyndale House Publishers, 1993), 45–63.

[63] Barbara Johnson, *Mama, Get the Hammer! There's a Fly on Papa's Head!* (Dallas: Word Publishing, 1994).

[64] Philip Yancey, "When God Seems Silent," *Today's Christian Woman*, March/April 1989, 28–30.

[65] Fred Price, "Keeping the Faith," *Charisma and Christian Life*, October 1988, 58–63.

[66] Ruth Vaughn, *Moody*, December 1998, 60–62.

[67] Rebecca Olson, "Building for Life," *Decision*, November 1987, 33–35.

[68] Ray Palmer, "My Faith Looks Up to Thee," 1830, public domain.

ABOUT THE AUTHOR

Stan Toler is senior pastor of Trinity Church of the Nazarene in Oklahoma City, Oklahoma, and for several years taught seminars for Dr. John Maxwell's INJOY Group, a leadership development institute. He has written over seventy books, including his best sellers, *God Has Never Failed Me, but He's Sure Scared Me to Death a Few Times; The Buzzards Are Circling, but God's Not Finished with Me Yet; God's Never Late, He's Seldom Early, He's Always Right on Time; The Secret Blend; Practical Guide to Pastoral Ministry; Total Quality Life*, and his popular Minute Motivator series. His latest book, *ReThink Your Life*, debuted at No. 23 on the CBA Christian Living Best Sellers list.

For additional information on seminars, to schedule speaking engagements, or to contact the author:

Stan Toler
P. O. Box 892170
Oklahoma City, OK 73189-2170
Email: stoler1107@aol.com
Web site: www.StanToler.com

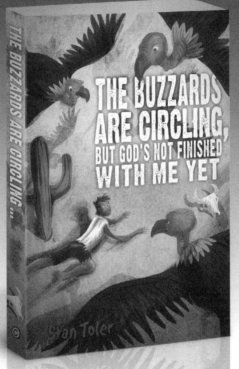